RAISING A GIRL WITH ADHD

RAISING A GIRL WITH ADHD

A PRACTICAL GUIDE TO HELP GIRLS HARNESS THEIR UNIQUE STRENGTHS AND ABILITIES

ALLISON K. TYLER, LCSW

ROCKRIDGE
PRESS

For general information on our other products and services or to obtain technical support, please contact our Customer Care Department within the United States at (866) 744-2665, or outside the United States at (510) 253-0500.

Rockridge Press publishes its books in a variety of electronic and print formats. Some content that appears in print may not be available in electronic books, and vice versa.

TRADEMARKS: Rockridge Press and the Rockridge Press logo are trademarks or registered trademarks of Callisto Media Inc. and/or its affiliates, in the United States and other countries, and may not be used without written permission. All other trademarks are the property of their respective owners. Rockridge Press is not associated with any product or vendor mentioned in this book.

Interior and Cover Designer: Richard Tapp
Photo Art Director/Art Manager: Sue Bischofberger
Editors: Meera Pal and John Makowski
Production Editor: Ashley Polikoff
Illustration © 2021 Remie Geoffroi, cover; Semanche/shutterstock.com, p. i; recurring pattern designed by Vilmosvarga/Freepik.com
Author photo courtesy of Erin Galardi/Ruffles and Trains Photography
ISBN: Print 978-1-64611-390-3 | eBook 978-1-64611-391-0
R0

To my daughter, Celeste.
As your name suggests, your effervescence reminds us all to aim for the stars.
Keep dreaming big, aiming high, and breaking down barriers.

CONTENTS

Introduction **viii**

PART ONE : ADHD 101   3

CHAPTER 1: Learning about Your Girl and ADHD   5

CHAPTER 2: Living with a Girl Who Has ADHD   23

PART TWO : MANAGING ADHD   37

CHAPTER 3: Managing ADHD Behaviors   39

CHAPTER 4: Girls with ADHD and Coexisting Conditions   55

PART THREE : THRIVING WITH ADHD   69

CHAPTER 5: Building Life Skills   71

CHAPTER 6: Tips for Success   81

Resources   **95**

References   **99**

Index   **103**

INTRODUCTION

am a licensed clinical social worker who has specialized in attention-deficit/hyperactivity disorder (ADHD) for most of my career. But, perhaps more important, I'm also the mother of a child with ADHD. So, I understand from a professional perspective and from a personal one how ADHD can affect children and families.

When I first started working with children with ADHD, many people believed that ADHD affected boys more than girls. But the truth is that ADHD is more often diagnosed in boys than in girls. It got me wondering why that is and what makes the presentation of ADHD symptoms in girls less obvious. At the time, there wasn't a ton of great research or information available about ADHD, and there definitely wasn't research about girls and ADHD. However, as a solo practitioner, I noted that the anecdotal evidence of parents I worked with highlighted a few key commonalities. I also read the groundbreaking book *Understanding Girls with ADHD*, written by some of the great women studying and researching ADHD: Kathleen Nadeau, Ellen Littman, and Patricia Quinn. This book helped me understand that girls' brains process information differently, which means that their ADHD symptoms may appear very differently. It's also important to understand that these differences aren't yet clinically documented in diagnostic criteria. So, even though we know that the research supports the fact that girls and boys may manifest ADHD symptoms differently, we are still using the same criteria to diagnose them.

***

Years ago, I knew a little girl who struggled with low self-esteem. She was smart, friendly, and full of energy and ideas. She did well socially and enjoyed trying new things, but she struggled with finishing projects, chores, and homework. To deal with her difficulties, she developed little systems to help herself. She wrote everything down on sticky notes and asked her parents for reminders. As she got older, her systems evolved. In college, when she had to wake up for an early class, she set two alarms. She also used silly songs to memorize information for exams.

That little girl was me. Of course, there were many things I wish I had known when I was young and many skills that would have benefited me. But I got through life because kids are resilient, and if there is one magic thing that girls with ADHD possess, it's resilience.

This book is intended to give you foundational information about how ADHD affects girls. I will provide strategies and problem-solving skills to use when you feel stuck or stressed out as a parent. An ADHD diagnosis means that your life may be a little different from what you expected, but don't despair. ADHD has many wondrous components, and we are only beginning to learn about the ways in which the female ADHD brain operates.

Getting the Most Out of This Book

This book is set up specifically so that you can turn to the section you need when you need it. I understand that, as a parent, you may sometimes feel stuck, and there may be a sense of urgency to look for help and support. Please don't feel like you have to start at the beginning and finish at the end. Start where you are. Right now. Today. So, if you need help in navigating homework issues, turn to page 44. Or if you are worried about your daughter's social experiences, turn to page 45. This book is designed to give you practical, hands-on help exactly when you need it. After reading this book, you should have a better understanding of what ADHD is and how it affects girls in different ways. You should also feel more confident in your parenting strategies and have an adequate supply of coping skills for both you and your daughter.

PART ONE: **ADHD 101**

LEARNING ABOUT YOUR GIRL AND ADHD

As parents, we don't have a magic book with all the answers. It's hard to know what to do when you have a daughter who may seem slightly different or faces struggles that appear unique. My goal is to help you feel more confident as a parent and instill some hope, levity, and support so that you can focus on your amazing girl with ADHD.

In this chapter, we are going to break down ADHD. We will define what it is and discuss some of the research about ADHD brains and the importance of early diagnosis and intervention. Then we are going to examine how ADHD looks different in girls and the possible reasons for the discrepancy between boys and girls. Finally, we will get into building your parenting tool kit by learning some new strategies to help you navigate those difficult moments.

Holding on to Unrealistic Expectations

We all enter parenthood with our own ideas, ideals, and fantasies about what parenthood will look like and who our children will be. And yet, our children are who they are, which may create dissonance with our own expectations. These expectations may come from our own idealized or treasured childhood experiences; alternatively, these ideas may exist in an attempt to craft a completely different experience for your children than your own. Oftentimes, the reality is just not close to what we have imagined. It doesn't mean that you don't have joys, happiness, or moments of pride and accomplishment. However, our reality is simply different from our expectations, which can be disappointing. For many of us, becoming a parent brings about many complex emotions, but being able to recognize those emotions when they get in the way is extremely important. When you have a daughter with ADHD, sometimes it's important to take a look at yourself and think about what expectations you can release so that you can create space for what is realistic and manageable. Being honest with yourself is a great way to create a better relationship with your child. One of the best strengths you can model for your daughter is the ability to adjust the expectations that you have for both your daughter and yourself.

ADHD in Girls Looks Different

ADHD is a neurodevelopmental disorder, which means it affects a child's brain, and symptoms usually become present during child development and growth. It's important to remember that every child may have a slightly different presentation of ADHD, so symptoms could vary slightly. That being said, some research is starting to emerge about why ADHD looks different in girls.

Understanding ADHD

So, what exactly is ADHD? Attention-deficit/hyperactivity disorder is a complex brain condition that is characterized by ongoing patterns of inattention, hyperactivity, and impulsivity.

There are three main types of ADHD: primarily hyperactive-impulsive, primarily inattentive (which was formerly referred to as ADD), and a combination of the first two types.

Type 1: Children with hyperactive-impulsive type ADHD tend to have trouble sitting still for long periods and act as if driven by a motor. They are often talkative, impulsive, and impatient, and they may interrupt others and have difficulty managing their emotions.

Meet Lexie:

Lexie is eight years old and is always going, going, going. She wakes up with big, big creative ideas and loves imaginative play. Her parents joke that she brings a hurricane with her wherever she goes. She changes clothes several times a day (leaving discarded clothes on the floor in her room), moves from one messy art project to the next very quickly, and has trouble not interrupting her parents when she has something important to say. Lexie has a lot of friends, but they sometimes get frustrated with her inability to listen to them, and, at times, Lexie can be inflexible when it comes to cooperative play and sharing. She is a big, shining light, and her energy is infectious. She loves to talk, laugh, and be silly, but when Lexie gets upset or frustrated, she tends to explode. She can easily go from laughing and joking to yelling and crying when faced with an unexpected disappointment or change of plans.

Type 2: Children with inattentive type ADHD are forgetful and easily distracted. They tend to daydream, struggle with staying organized in tasks and sequential behavior sequences, have poor time management, and avoid activities that require sustained mental effort (such as homework).

Meet Georgie:

Georgie is 10 years old. She's quiet, bright, and thoughtful. She's done well in school until recently, in fifth grade, when she started changing classes. Her teachers have noticed that she tends to daydream a lot. When she was younger and invited to birthday parties, Georgie was shy and would often play by herself or stay with the adults. Georgie loves horses, and she loves playing *Star Stable* (an online horse game). She is a homebody and loves reading Harriet the Spy books, watching *StoryBots*, and being with her cats. Lately, her parents have noticed that she has been forgetting assignments and struggling with making careless mistakes on quizzes and tests at school. Georgie has a few close friends, but she tends to be shy at first and does best in one-on-one social situations.

Type 3: Children with the combined type of ADHD exhibit behaviors from both hyperactive-impulsive and inattentive types, and their symptoms don't fall into either of the first two types. Most children fall in this category.

Meet Kiara:

Kiara is 14 years old and in eighth grade. As a young child, she was very active physically, and her parents placed her in gymnastics, where she excelled. She puts all of her energy into her competitions and feels her best when she is doing gymnastics. Kiara has lots of friends but can be very bossy and opinionated. Her mother has had several calls from her school over the years about Kiara having social issues during recess. At school, Kiara feels like she is "stupid" because it takes her a lot longer to understand material when she reads, and she has an IEP (individualized education plan) to help with her dyslexia. Kiara is becoming much more aware of her looks and spends a lot of time deciding what to wear. Kiara sometimes feels like she doesn't fit in and would like to be more accepted by her peers. She has never had a "best friend."

ADHD in Girls

If you think your daughter has ADHD, you should consult with your daughter's pediatrician and discuss the options. Most doctors will refer you to a child and adolescent board certified psychiatrist or a developmental pediatrician to have your daughter evaluated. There isn't a simple test that experts use to diagnose a child with ADHD. Because the symptoms of ADHD can overlap with other disorders, doctors will often rule out depression, anxiety, or sleep disorders.

The American Psychiatric Association's *Diagnostic and Statistical Manual of Mental Disorders* (*DSM-5*) includes a diagnostic evaluation used to assess children and adults. The evaluation process usually consists of a combination of interviewing parents, interviewing your child, and having you or your daughter's teacher fill out a form (such as the Vanderbilt ADHD Diagnostic Rating Scale).

The APA's *DSM-5* lists nine symptoms that help doctors determine the type of ADHD a child may be exhibiting. There are nine for ADHD primarily inattentive, and nine for ADHD primarily hyperactive-impulsive. According to *ADDitude* magazine, a child must have exhibited at least six of the nine symptoms for six months, showing up in more than one environment—school and home—in order to receive an ADHD diagnosis.

By using all the information collected, the doctor will make a diagnosis and suggest a treatment plan, which could include behavioral therapy and medication.

An estimated 8.4 percent of all children have ADHD, according to the American Psychiatric Association, and it's thought to be as prevalent in girls as in boys. But it is still underdiagnosed in girls. Current statistics from the CDC show that boys are more likely to be diagnosed with ADHD than girls (12.9 percent for boys compared to 5.6 percent for girls).

For most people, ADHD is genetic, which means it's usually inherited from a parent. The specific genes that cause ADHD are yet to be isolated. In fact, it's very common for parents to realize that they have ADHD when they are going through the process of having their child diagnosed.

According to Children and Adults with Attention-Deficit/Hyperactivity Disorder (CHADD), other potential causes include exposure to smoking and alcohol, certain chemicals and pesticides, and premature birth or low birth weight.

How and Why ADHD Manifests Differently in Girls

It's hard to know exactly why ADHD shows up differently in girls than it does in boys because there isn't enough research on ADHD in women and girls. Many clinicians suspect that part of the reason may be that boys with hyperactive elements of ADHD tend to display more extreme behavior than girls. Professionals believe that girls tend to develop more coping skills that hide some of the symptoms, such as putting most of their focus into an activity in which they are highly skilled. The American Psychological Association notes that because girls with ADHD tend to exhibit more inattentive type ADHD symptoms than hyperactive-impulsive type ADHD symptoms, they are often underdiagnosed. Girls with ADHD tend to display slightly different symptoms, such as shyness, difficulty making social connections or reading social cues, daydreaming, anxiety, picking at their skin, or being perfectionists about their work. These differences are often missed by teachers, caregivers, and parents.

The Power of Early Intervention

Research suggests that undiagnosed girls with ADHD are at risk of low self-esteem, underachievement, and other disorders (such as depression and anxiety). Without intervention, undiagnosed girls will carry these problems with them into adulthood.

Early intervention, or early diagnosis and treatment, can go a long way toward helping girls live with ADHD and lead happy, successful lives. Not only can it help you adjust your parenting, but it can also give you the ability to understand your child better. You can get to know what your daughter needs, what her strengths and weaknesses are, and how they affect her in different situations.

For example, your daughter may be an amazing soccer player—put her on the field, and she is in her element—but she may also struggle in the classroom or have difficulty reading social cues in small group settings. Having this information will help you become a better advocate for your child in these situations, and it can also help you adjust her expectations, practice new skills, and problem-solve more effectively. Additionally, children with ADHD often need some extra help at school, and they may benefit from certain services, such as assistance from a paraprofessional, occupational therapy, and small-setting instructional time.

Behavioral Strategies for Parents

I always tell parents that they need to have a fully stocked tool kit for their parenting needs. In 17 years of working with children and parents, I have learned that being consistent is just as important as being flexible. Sometimes, as a parent, you may try a strategy that works great, and then you try it again, and it does nothing. In that situation, what do you do? Well, you can try again, or you can try a different strategy. There are so many reasons why a strategy works or fails, but having a good rotation of problem-solving approaches can keep you, as the parent, feeling confident and in control. Remember that oftentimes, when we want to de-escalate a conflict, we need to do the opposite of what our natural impulses are telling us. So, if you want to yell, lower your voice instead. If you want to get closer, take a step back. And if you want to immediately punish, take a break and some time to think.

Let's talk about some strategies that you can start to implement with your daughter to help manage or avoid difficult moments.

Verbal Cues: Positivity, Praise, and Effective Instructions

You may notice that communicating with your daughter can be frustrating or confusing. You may have to repeat instructions over and over. Or your daughter may become very easily irritated or upset by just a simple question or request. For example, who knew asking your child to hang up their backpack would unleash such wrath? Because ADHD affects the ways in which information is received and interpreted, creating effective communication styles for your ADHD girl is extremely important.

Keeping Things Positive

Many experts, including psychiatrist and leading ADHD specialist Dr. William Dodson, estimate that children with ADHD receive, on average, 20,000 more negative messages than other children. Some emerging research shows that children with ADHD may be more sensitive to criticism and, as a result, avoid situations in which they anticipate negative feedback. So, it's important to be mindful of the ways in which we address children with ADHD. Keeping things as positive, or even more positive, than usual may help balance out messages received by your child. How do you do this? Consider simple changes in the way you speak to your child. It's not about making everything sound flowery and artificial, but sending messages that imbue confidence.

INSTEAD OF	TRY
Please don't climb on the couch.	You seem to need to move. Should we do some jumping jacks together?
Stop grabbing from your sister.	I wonder if it's possible to find another baby doll.
Calm down.	I hear you are upset. Let's find a quiet place to talk.
If you don't stop, then . . .	I see this is hard. Let's find a different way.
Why are you acting like this?	You are feeling strong feelings.

Shower Them with Praise

The importance of praise can't be overestimated. Girls with ADHD need us to give them motivating, inspiring, and loving feedback. Just like with positivity, think about praise as an underused condiment in the recipe of parenting. Pepper it into everything you do. Here are some examples of how to incorporate more praise for your daughter:

- **Recognize the efforts as well as the end result.** "Wow, I can see how much work you are putting into studying for your Spanish test."

- **Make observations in the present.** Instead of saying "good job" or "well done," notice and observe a detail about your child. For instance, "The brush strokes you are painting in your art project really stand out."

- **Praise moments of social interaction, as well as academic and sports achievements.** "Your friends really enjoyed the games you chose today."

- **Don't forget nonverbal praise.** Giving your child a subtle wink, thumbs-up, high five, or smile when you see that they are trying can go a long way.

Giving Effective Instructions

You may be noticing a theme here, but sometimes packaging and delivering information differently can result in better outcomes for your girl. Giving instructions can be one of those moments. ADHD affects executive function skills—specifically the ability to plan and prioritize things—so organizing your words clearly can help boost your daughter's ability to follow instructions logically.

- **Be specific.** Instead of saying "go get ready for school," give your child specific directions, such as "brush your teeth" or "get dressed in the clothes laid out on your bed." The younger your child is, the fewer instructions her brain can handle.

- **Be concise.** Less is more. Give one instruction and ask them to check back in with you when it's completed.

- **Make a routine of it.** For instructions that relate to a particular routine, such as morning or bedtime, try to encourage your child to do tasks in the same order. This will help get them sealed into memory.

- **Write all routines down.** Having a central place with routines listed is a great way to remind your child what to do, what comes next, and what to prioritize.

Discipline

When I was a young and inexperienced therapist in the early 2000s, I read Dr. Ross W. Greene's *The Explosive Child,* and I was blown away by his philosophy about child behavior. In it, he explains that "kids do the best they can with the skills they have." In other words, when we see negative behaviors in children, such as a meltdown, it's not because they are being manipulative or trying to get their way. It's because their skill set is not yet evolved enough to deal with the situation they are currently experiencing. It made so much sense to me as a therapist who worked with young children.

If you ever watch a child having a meltdown, you'll notice it's extremely unpleasant for them. It's a total loss of control, humiliating, exhausting, and often seems frightening for the child to experience. In my 17 years of work as a therapist and nine years as a mother of a child with ADHD, I've learned that the best discipline you can give your daughter with ADHD is to strengthen her problem-solving skills. This is best done by teaching and modeling. For this reason, I don't believe in time-outs or behavior charts. These tools only serve to let our children know what will happen when their skill set is exhausted. Instead, let's discuss how to de-escalate situations by adjusting expectations and teaching calming strategies.

- **Don't sweat the small stuff.** It's not earth-shattering or anything you haven't heard before, but it's one of the best and most effective pieces of advice I can give to parents of kids with ADHD. Let the little things go. What does this mean? Well, is it a travesty if your daughter wears the same T-shirt that she did yesterday? Is it really worth imposing your will on her? By being more flexible with your parenting, you are modeling flexibility for your daughter.

- **Use distraction.** This usually works well with younger children. But at the first sign of agitation (and you likely know exactly what this looks like in your daughter), try "changing the channel." You can do this by making an environmental change (moving to a different room or playing some favorite music).

- **Don't make demands.** Resist the urge to "turn up the volume" on the situation. When your daughter begins to show signs of her diminished skill set, you can't expect her to meet a demand. Think about escalation like a wave that your child is riding—you can either jump in and ride it with her as it rises, or you can stay on land and offer her a lifeline.

- **Decrease stimulation if escalation continues.** Remember that your daughter's brain is different; it sends and receives information differently and sometimes inconsistently. Dim the lights, have others leave the room quietly, and turn down the music or TV.

- **Practice using nonjudgmental language.** Telling your daughter that she is acting like a baby or trying to embarrass her won't help the situation. Remember that she is already probably not feeling great about herself in this moment. Using harsh language or judgments may only serve to send her self-esteem downward.

- **Listen to and reflect your daughter's views verbally.** Making sure to verbalize your daughter's point of view is extremely important because it teaches her that her feelings are valid. While you may not agree with what is happening, what your child is feeling is her reality. Reflect back and restate to her what she says calmly.

Calming Strategies

Teaching your daughter ways to calm herself down is going to take some trial and error. You may find that one strategy works in one situation but not in another. That's why it's good to arm yourself with a slew of ideas that you can throw at the problem when it arises.

- **Deep breathing.** One way I practice this is when I see a child beginning to get upset or escalate, I say nothing and begin to take deep breaths in through my nose and out through my mouth. More often than not, after a few breaths, I can get the child to join in with me.

- **Take them on a walk outside**. Fresh air can work wonders. Even a walk around the block can offer a physical outlet for frustration.

- **Have your child listen to music with headphones.** Allowing your daughter to really immerse herself in music can offer an escape from intense feelings, as well as create an outlet.

- **Try the balloon technique.** Have your daughter blow up a balloon and allow her to pop it. This can be an effective strategy for kids who tend to be more physical or destructive when they get emotionally stuck.

- **Offer up some pet snuggles.** If you have a pet, they can be great for calming down intense emotions.

- **Give them alone time or special one-on-one time.** Some kids benefit greatly from taking some quiet time by themselves, while others need their parents near them when they feel intense emotions.

- **Use visually calming stimulation.** Playing a video of waves crashing or offering a calming glitter jar or lava lamp can help a child reorganize their emotions and feel more at ease.

- **Put on a short yoga video.** Find a two- to three-minute yoga video on YouTube. Sometimes doing yoga can help slow things down. Going upside down (or into downward dog) can help stimulate your child's vestibular system, which can have a calming effect.

Plan Ahead

Part of parenting a girl with ADHD is getting to know her and anticipating problems or issues before they happen. Planning ahead will be one of your best parenting strategies, and eventually, it's something that you'll want your daughter to do for herself. There are a couple of ways to do this to optimize best outcomes and minimize meltdowns, tears, and frustration.

Pick Appropriate Activities

Whether it's sports, music, or deciding whether or not to RSVP to a birthday party, picking the right activities for your child is a good way to maximize success. Of course, it's easier said than done, and there is always some trial and error with making these choices. But you are the expert on your daughter, so trust your intuition—it's usually right. That being said, here are some guidelines and tips to help you:

- **Know your child's strengths.** If your daughter is physically bold, a risk-taker, and enjoys lots of physical and sensory movement, she may be great at rock climbing, track, hockey, tennis, swimming, or tae kwon do. However, she may struggle with baseball (which requires more patience and waiting) or dance (which requires following detailed instructions).

- **Consider the coach/teacher/leader.** Whether it's sports, scouting, or cheerleading, having an understanding coach or teacher is important to your daughter's success. Make sure you meet the coach beforehand and have a conversation with them. Give them some information about your daughter and her ADHD and how you help her when she gets upset or stuck. If you don't have a good feeling about the coach or they aren't receptive to your conversation, consider looking elsewhere.

- **Don't overdo it.** It may seem like trying to tire out your daughter with a packed schedule is a good strategy, but make sure you plan enough downtime for her to relax and unwind. ADHD brains need plenty of rest.

Visual Schedules and Checklists

A visual schedule is a picture-based or graphic representation of scheduled events and activities. Having a visual schedule for younger ADHD girls is a great way to help them understand their routine and know what's coming. It can also help them start to independently learn sequences and prepare for highly anticipated activities that are out of the ordinary (like vacations, birthday parties, and holidays). Consider putting one in a high-traffic area of your home, where it will be seen on a daily basis, such as your kitchen or your daughter's bedroom. Some parents prepare a few schedules for daily routines and place them strategically around the home. For example, a bathroom routine can go up on your child's bathroom mirror.

DAILY SCHEDULE

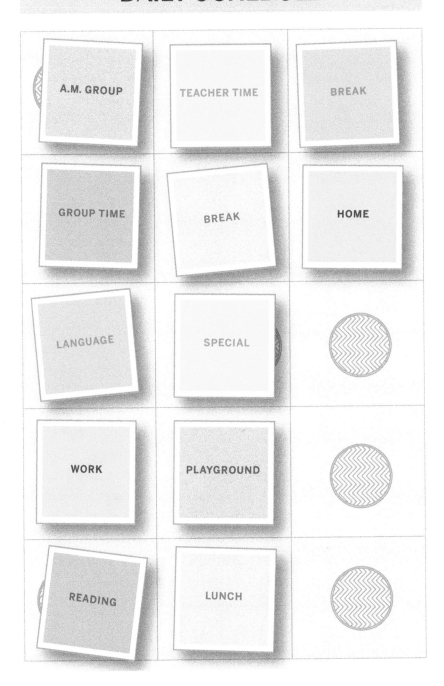

A.M. GROUP

TEACHER TIME

BREAK

GROUP TIME

BREAK

HOME

LANGUAGE

SPECIAL

WORK

PLAYGROUND

READING

LUNCH

Checklists for older ADHD girls can achieve the same result. You can create them for your daughter's common routines (homework, backpack, bedtime, sports practice, etc.) and help her start creating her own.

SWIM TEAM BAG:
☐   Towel
☐   Bathing suit
☐   Sweats
☐   Swim cap
☐   Goggles

Managing Expectations

The anticipation of exciting, happy, new events (such as parties, holidays, and vacations) can sometimes overstimulate girls with ADHD, which increases the likelihood of meltdowns and disappointment. You may notice this and dread getting a birthday party invitation or worry about the upcoming Halloween party in your daughter's class. Sometimes these unusual occurrences create system overloads, so giving your daughter the opportunity to think about and prepare for them beforehand can be extremely helpful. Be sure to discuss each event with your daughter in advance and let her know what the schedule/routine for that particular day will be. Ask her what her expectations are, and be clear with her about what is realistic and what isn't.

Takeaways

In this chapter, we've covered what ADHD is, the statistics research, and some information about the ADHD brain. We've also looked at what is different about girls with ADHD and why their presentation may be different from boys'. We then progressed to some specific strategies you can start using with your girl. Remember to keep updating your tool kit and come back to this section if you are feeling frustrated or burned out. Remember that your flexibility is just as important as your consistency. In the next chapter, we'll move on to what living with a girl with ADHD is like and how to tackle some of those everyday problems.

Chapter 1 Cheat Sheet:

- Let go of unrealistic parenting expectations that no longer serve you or your daughter.

- There are three types of ADHD: hyperactive-impulsive, inattentive, and combined.

- Early intervention after diagnosis of ADHD leads to better outcomes.

- Keep working on building up your parenting tool kit by using positive language, giving effective instructions, and thinking about discipline differently.

- Make use of de-escalation and calming strategies.

- Use visual schedules and checklists.

LIVING WITH A GIRL WHO HAS ADHD

N ow let's dive into the day-to-day information you will need to thrive with your daughter with ADHD. We are going to discuss how ADHD presents differently in girls, the variances in language issues, and the challenges of living with a girl with ADHD. I'll also highlight some tips and tricks to help you and your other children communicate more effectively with your daughter.

ADHD Isn't One-Size-Fits-All

It can be frustrating as a parent of a girl with ADHD because you may feel that some of the common criteria for ADHD presents differently in your daughter. For this reason, it may have taken longer to get this diagnosis or for professionals to take your concerns seriously. Let's take a look at how ADHD can present differently.

Hyperactive/Impulsive

In general, the hyperactive-impulsive type of ADHD (type 1) is described as children who are extremely physically active and have difficulty sitting still, keeping their hands to themselves, and controlling their impulses. In girls, however, this may look slightly different. For example, some girls may hyperfocus their physical activity into a passion, such as a sport or dancing. Your child may be labeled a tomboy, and her excellence in her physical performance may overshadow other ADHD symptoms. Another manifestation is the talkative, highly social child. Your daughter may be extremely conversational and seek stimulation through verbal feedback. You may notice that she is prone to frequent verbal interruptions or often changes the topic of conversation. Additionally, these characteristics may lead to your daughter being prone to social drama.

Let's revisit Lexie:

Lexie had rough day today at school. She had her name written on the board by her teacher for talking and interrupting in class too much. During recess, she had an argument with friends who became frustrated with her for trying to tell everyone what roles they were playing in their tag game. After school, she had play practice, where she really shines. She loves the music and the combination of movement in the dance routines and singing her heart out. Her play director gave her a speaking part this year, and she loves practicing her lines. Unfortunately, remembering to bring home her science book is another story completely.

Inattentive/Distractible

Girls with inattentive type ADHD (type 2) may also hyperfocus their energy into one area that they excel in. This focus on excellence may prevent people, such as teachers and parents, from seeing other symptoms, such as daydreaming, distractibility, and difficulty focusing. In general, this type of ADHD usually takes longer to get diagnosed because the symptoms are less apparent or extreme. They are also less disruptive and tend to affect the child internally, as opposed to disrupting their environment outwardly, as with hyperactivity.

Shy/Withdrawn

Inattentive type ADHD can sometimes appear as though your daughter is quiet, shy, or withdrawn. Her distractions may be more inward, so she may be labeled as a loner.

When Georgie was younger, she was painfully shy. She would cry end-lessly at preschool drop-off and even had a hard time separating at the start of kindergarten. It's slowly getting easier, but Georgie doesn't always feel comfortable talking. She can often be seen sitting quietly on the periphery of social groups, listening and observing.

Perfectionist/Obsessive/Anxious

Children with both inattentive and hyperactive-impulsive type ADHD may exhibit signs of perfectionism or have particular obsessions. How does this play out in everyday life? Your daughter may get hung up on very specific details when doing homework or hyperfocus on a particu-lar subject in which she is interested. She may get fixated or stuck on a deadline or a highly anticipated event, such as a party, playdate, or holi-day. For some, this anticipation may tip into anxiety, which may lead to some people labeling your daughter as sensitive or a worrier.

Let's revisit Kiara:

Remember Kiara? She has recently started going to higher-level competitions for gymnastics. This sometimes involves traveling and staying overnight at hotels, which she loves. She has also been exposed to more gymnasts. Seeing the competition outperform her makes her really driven to improve her gymnastic skills. However, her mother notices that she can sometimes obsess about her progress and be really hard on herself when she doesn't meet her own very high expectations.

Language Development and Processing

With time, your daughter's language skills will progress and become more complex both in the ways she expresses herself and how she inter-prets others. Keep in mind that there are a few learning issues that can affect language and language development in girls with ADHD.

Auditory Processing

According to a January 2020 article in *ADDitude* magazine, recent studies illustrate that about half of all children diagnosed with ADHD also have auditory processing disorder (APD). APD is a brain disorder that makes it hard for children to distinguish between two distinct sounds, and they may be easily distracted by background noises or have difficulty processing thoughts. Auditory processing disorder can present similarly to ADHD, which is why it's important to have your daughter tested by a qualified audiologist to rule it out.

Children with APD often become more agitated or frustrated during learning periods when there is more noise. It may also appear like the child isn't understanding or is misunderstanding information. They may also choose to disengage and become disruptive or distracted.

Experts don't know for certain what causes APD or why it is correlated so highly with ADHD, but it may be caused by Lyme disease, exposure to heavy metals, or other brain injuries. There is good news, which is that auditory pathways continue to develop into adolescence, so with early intervention, APD can be treated successfully.

Expressive and Receptive Language Skills

One out of every 10 children diagnosed with ADHD have a speech problem, such as articulation, stuttering, or difficulty with word or sound pronunciation. Expressive language skills are skills that help a child speak and be understood. Receptive language skills are the ability to listen to and understand what is being communicated.

The prevalence of speech issues can cause a disruption in expressive language skills and can lead to children feeling frustrated when they aren't understood. Additionally, it can lead to social misunderstandings or misreadings. What does this look like? Children with ADHD tend to use more word fillers or repetitions as they process and organize their thoughts. This can lead to a stammer or to losing their audience as other children may become impatient.

If you think that your child may have a speech issue, reach out to a local professional to have her evaluated. Many times, if a speech issue is affecting your daughter in school, this evaluation can be done through the school.

Literacy Development

Fifty percent of children with ADHD also struggle with a learning disability. The most common learning disabilities in children with ADHD are:

- **Dyslexia (difficulty reading):** More specifically, dyslexia refers to the brain's struggle to decipher different letters and sounds. It can be very difficult for someone with dyslexia to break down words into separate speech sounds, and, conversely, it can be very challenging to blend together new sounds. Children diagnosed with dyslexia require different forms of instruction in reading and phonics. Symptoms or signs of dyslexia include difficulty learning to talk; difficulty learning the alphabet or a sequence of numbers, colors, etc.; difficulty with rhyming; and difficulty learning sounds and letter names.

- **Dysgraphia (difficulty writing):** Dysgraphia is a problem of the nervous system that affects the development of skills that help a child write. Symptoms of dysgraphia include having unclear or inconsistent handwriting, difficulty copying text, and writing very slowly. Other signs include a cramped grip, frequent erasing, and unusual paper or wrist position while writing. Children diagnosed with dysgraphia may need assistance from an occupational thera-pist to help strengthen their fine motor skills. They may also benefit from certain assistive technology aids, such as voice-to-text dicta-tion software, use of video or audio reports to help with studying, and the use of a computer.

- **Dyscalculia (difficulty with math computations):** Dyscalculia is a fancy word that describes a math learning disability. It may look like difficulty doing math computations; difficulty comprehending math reasoning; trouble remembering and applying math rules, formulas, and strategies; and difficulty memorizing math facts. Experts believe that a math learning disability is more common in children with ADHD due to deficits in the executive function skill of working memory. Working memory is the ability to hold on to and manipulate information in your brain (such as doing mental math). For many with ADHD, working memory deficits lead to difficulty with math computations.

It's important to remember that learning disabilities may present differently in children. For example, your child may refuse to do work or avoid work that is difficult for them due to a disability. Alternatively, they may not avoid the work at all, but may be progressing at a much slower rate or below their potential due to their disability. Additionally, disruptive behaviors may be more present in the classroom when your child is presented with work that is impacted by their disability.

Executive Function

You may have heard the term "executive functions" in relation to your daughter's ADHD diagnosis. The brain uses executive function skills to help you organize and access information and emotions. They are the ability to plan, prioritize, organize, control impulses and emotions, think flexibly, initiate tasks, access working memory, and self-monitor. Almost all children diagnosed with ADHD lack or have deficits in some or all of the executive functions. These deficits result in the symptoms that we see in girls with ADHD, such as impulsive behavior, difficulty focusing, lack of concentration, trouble staying on task, and difficulty following a sequence of instructions. Emotionally, the lack of executive function skills can manifest in your daughter as a low frustration tolerance, social inflexibility, and trouble reading social cues.

Plan: This is the ability to look ahead and make decisions appropriately regarding scheduling and time management. You may see deficits in this executive function skill in girls who have difficulty managing time. It may look like a girl who starts a long-term assignment the night before it's due or underestimating the amount of time a project will take.

Prioritize: This is the ability to look at tasks and organize them according to importance. In my work with girls with ADHD, I see this deficit in kids when they are unable to plan ahead for longer-term assignments or work on the most important item on their to-do list.

Organize: This is the ability to create systems to keep belongings and information in order. Does your daughter have a messy room, backpack, or both? Does she struggle with losing things and keeping organizational systems intact?

Emotional regulation: This is the ability to regulate emotions so that reactions match the size of the problem. It may look like a huge overreaction, inability to calm down after getting upset, or overzealousness when it comes to following the rules of a game or feeling cheated or wronged.

Initiate tasks: This is the ability to create a clear intention for a task and follow through on it without distraction. Your daughter may know that she has a paper due in a week, but sitting down and starting the task seems impossible. She'll go to her room, sit at her computer, and stare out the window or end up browsing at her favorite online store.

Access working memory: Working memory is the ability to hold on to and manipulate information in your brain. Working memory requires an inner brain "clipboard" on which you can copy and save information to use for future problem-solving. Multitasking requires a lot of working memory strength, so remembering multistep directions can be difficult. This may also look like quickly forgetting something that was just mentioned, or remembering part of an instruction but not the entire instruction.

Think flexibly: This is the ability to pick up on cues and adapt accordingly. Group cooperation, sharing, compromising, and admitting mistakes or wrongdoing may be challenging if your daughter has difficulty with thinking flexibly.

Self-reflection: This is the inability to take responsibility for wrongdoing—or difficulty adjusting behavior correctively—after realizing a mistake. This may look like repeating the same mistake over and over. It may also look like your daughter is intentionally engaging in self-destructive behavior.

Living Together

Having a daughter with ADHD may mean that you have to change or reevaluate your parenting style slightly, and that's okay. It can also be difficult to parent one child differently than another. This may sometimes lead to feelings of guilt or shame as a parent, but I encourage you to let go of these judgments and embrace the freedom of parenting flexibly. Different types of children may need different patterns and different strategies. It's perfectly okay, it's perfectly healthy, and it's perfectly normal. Sometimes making dynamic shifts in the way that you relate to your child can make all the difference in keeping and maintaining a healthy household.

Tips for Parents

- **Be clear with your expectations.** Communicate with your child clearly and directly and make your expectations concise and age appropriate. Reconsider lengthy lectures or tangents because you are most likely going to lose your child's attention very quickly.

- **Have consistent routines.** Girls with ADHD need extra prompts to stay organized. Maintaining regular routines for morning, evening, and bedtime helps enforce sequenced driven behaviors.

- **Allow for flexibility when it comes to discipline.** Children with ADHD get way more negative feedback than children without ADHD. Redirection, teaching new skills, and positive parenting are techniques that are going to get you more bang for your buck than harsh parenting.

- **Don't make comparisons.** Comparing your daughter to your friend's children or your other children isn't fair to your daughter. It's okay to parent children with different needs differently.

- **Be patient and adjust your expectations.** Some skills are developmental with ADHD and may just come in time.

Tips for Siblings

- **Explain and educate siblings about ADHD and how it affects your daughter.** The more that siblings understand your daughter's ADHD, the more flexible you can expect them to be.

- **Give your other children some strategies to use in challenging situations.** For example, when your daughter is behaving impulsively or isn't listening, show her siblings what they can try to do. Give them a couple of examples, such as walking away for a few minutes and trying again when their sister is feeling calm.

- **Create opportunities for positive experiences and bonding.** For example, if your daughter's sibling is a strong athlete in soccer, ask if they can teach their sister some tips and tricks for ball handling. Conversely, ask your daughter with ADHD to teach her sibling how to get to the next level in *Mario Kart* or something else she's good at.

Lexie and Her Sister:

Lexie and her sister, Lucy, are playing UNO. Lexie begins to get very upset when she sees that her sister is about to win. Lexie was doing so well, and she was absolutely sure that she was going to be the victor. Once she makes this realization, she immediately throws her cards down and states that her sister must be cheating and refuses to play anymore. After a couple of minutes, Lucy gathers up her cards and asks Lexie if she would like to learn her strategy. Lexie agrees and apologizes for getting so upset. Lucy has learned that when Lexie gets upset, it's best to give her a few minutes to calm down before talking to her. She knows that when she gives Lexie a cooling period, they can usually problem-solve together.

Kiara and Her Sister:

Kiara likes to borrow her older sister's clothes, but she often takes them without asking. Unfortunately, not only will she forget to return them, but she has a history of leaving them in a heap on her bedroom floor or staining them carelessly. Kiara's sister is fed up and tells her that she has put a lock on her closet and will no longer allow Kiara to borrow her clothes. Upon hearing this, Kiara flies into a rage and begins calling her sister names and criticizing her with hurtful words. After this incident, the girls sit down with their parents to discuss what happened. Kiara, feeling remorseful, apologizes to her sister and explains that she loves her style and wants to learn how to dress like her. The two girls agree that they will go shopping together, and Kiara's sister will give her sister some fashion tips.

Parents, You Can Do This

It can be very challenging to have a daughter with ADHD. Some days can be draining and frustrating, and it can be really hard to watch your child struggle. While it may be tempting to take a defeatist attitude, staying rational and positive will fuel more successful interactions.

As much as we need to be our child's cheerleader and advocate, we also have to encourage ourselves. Parents are doing more than ever these days, so the fact that you are taking the time to read this book and work on yourself and your relationship with your daughter is already a step toward growth and improvement. As Wayne Gretzky said, "You miss 100 percent of the shots you don't take."

Takeaways

You should now have a better understanding of the various presentations of ADHD in girls and the ways in which learning issues can also affect them. I also highlighted some general tips and tricks for both parents and siblings to help make your household as harmonious as possible. In part 2, we will get into the everyday challenges of managing ADHD behaviors and symptoms.

Chapter 2 Cheat Sheet:

- The different types of ADHD play out differently in behaviors and presentation.

- Language issues, such as auditory processing issues, dyslexia, and literacy issues, are prevalent in girls with ADHD.

- Executive function skills help your daughter's brain organize and access her emotions. It's important to understand your daughter's deficits in executive function skills so that you can help her strengthen them.

PART TWO: **MANAGING ADHD**

MANAGING ADHD BEHAVIORS

Now let's get into what living at home with your daughter with ADHD looks like. We will cover some of the challenging moments, such as bedtime, mealtime, and playdates, and then we will start to look at supporting your daughter at school.

Managing Life at Home

Home life can be challenging with a girl with ADHD. The hardest moments can include times of transition (mealtimes and bedtimes); managing issues that come up with your daughter socially, such as friendships and playdates, can be equally difficult. I'm going to offer you some tips and strategies to help you keep these times as peaceful as possible.

Bedtime

Younger children with ADHD may have a difficult time winding down and resist going to bed because it feels uncomfortable. I have a few tips that can help:

- **Have a consistent, mutually agreed-upon bedtime.** This is key to reducing arguments and resistance about the actual time. Pick a time that is realistic for both your daughter and your family. Use a visual schedule reminder or a timer to help your daughter know when bedtime is approaching.

- **Create a calming bedtime routine.** Encourage your daughter to engage in quiet activities, such as reading, drawing, yoga, journaling, or listening to music or an audiobook. These cues can help induce sleepiness for children who struggle with sleep issues. If possible, eliminate screen time at least 30 minutes before bed.

- **Be flexible.** Sometimes it's okay to bend the rules a little bit. Allowing some flexibility for busy nights when everyone is stretched is fine, and it teaches your daughter to bend a little as well.

Mealtimes

Family meals are supposed to be the time for everyone to come together and catch up on their day, but they can be difficult for kids who have a hard time staying seated. Here are a few tips to keep your meals as enjoyable as possible for everyone:

- **Make the conversation fun by playing games.** Have a stack of silly questions to ask one another over dinner.

- **Recruit a helper.** Many girls with ADHD enjoy independence and the satisfaction of helping with chores. Enlist your daughter's help with cooking, setting the table, or selecting the music.

- **Keep it short.** Some kids really have a hard time staying seated, so expecting them to sit for 30 minutes for a meal is just not realistic. Give yourself permission to have shorter meals and excuse your child when she finishes if she can no longer be a productive part of the mealtime.

Playdates

Playdates can be tricky for younger children with ADHD. You may have had a bad experience with playdates and, consequently, either dread them or feel inclined to avoid them entirely. The truth is that all children benefit from learning how to socialize in less structured environments. There are a few ways to help ensure your daughter has a successful playdate:

- **Practice play planning with your daughter.** Before your daughter has a playdate, discuss with her what she would like to play and various scenarios that could take place. Help her foresee problems by asking questions like "I wonder if we should put your American Girl doll away since you have only one and it might be hard to share. What do you think?"

- **Keep the playdate shorter.** Start with scheduling shorter playdates. Have your daughter invite a friend over for an hour. Allow them to do an activity, have a snack, and then be done. Having shorter, successful playdates can help build everyone's confidence levels. As your daughter begins to get the hang of it, you can slowly increase the length of the playdate.

- **Model problem-solving.** If your daughter encounters an issue on the playdate, you may be inclined to immediately end it, but use the opportunity to help her develop her problem-solving skills. For example, if your daughter insists on choosing the movie to watch, ask her to come up with a list of three movies and let her friend choose from that list.

Managing Life at School

For some families, managing school and all that comes with it can be the most challenging endeavor. You may find that your daughter with ADHD holds it together during the day but falls apart as soon as she comes home, which makes everything after school very difficult. Or she may have negative associations with school and resists going or doing homework. Working with your daughter as her teammate instead of her adversary is going to help her feel supported and more willing to receive advice and support.

Advocating for Your Daughter

You are the expert on your daughter, which makes you her best advocate. One of the best ways to advocate for your daughter at school is to establish a good rapport with her teacher and create open avenues for communication. Make sure to reach out at the beginning of the academic year and let your daughter's teacher know what has worked for her in other classroom settings, what motivates her, and what she finds challenging. In addition, ask your daughter's teacher how you can best support them. Establishing these lines of communication early on will help you and your daughter's teacher be members of the same team.

Accommodations to Request

Accommodations are changes in education made to remove learning barriers. They are given to those with disabilities or special needs in school.

IEP/504

Accommodations can usually be made via two routes: either the Individuals with Disabilities Education Act (IDEA) or Section 504 of the Rehabilitation Act. Depending on which route best meets your daughter's needs, she will either have an IEP (individualized education plan) or a 504 plan. Both of these require a special meeting with specific members of your daughter's school, such as her teacher, school psychologist, speech therapist, occupational therapist, or a learning disability teaching consultant. The following is a list of some common accommodations given to children with ADHD. For a full list, visit the Resources section of the book on page 95.

Study partner/peer tutoring: Pairing your daughter with a positive peer-study role model can be helpful in supporting her to learn new study habits. Make sure it's someone with whom she has a good rapport. If your daughter is older, ask her teachers for suggestions of students who may be good study partners outside of school.

Quiet workspaces/alternative test settings: Some children with ADHD benefit greatly from taking tests or doing focus-intensive work in an alternative setting, such as a cubicle or quiet library; they may even benefit from using noise-canceling headphones to minimize distractions. Explore with your child's teacher whether your child might benefit from this accommodation.

Breaking down assignments: Large assignments, such as papers, projects, and book reports, can be overwhelming for all children. Kids with ADHD in particular may struggle with where to start sequentially and how to break down the assignment into realistic goals. Having larger assignments organized into smaller, digestible pieces can make the work much more attainable and accessible.

Movement breaks: Movement breaks, or sensory breaks, can be incredibly helpful, especially for children who struggle with staying seated. A knowledgeable teacher will know how to incorporate movement breaks in more discreet ways (such as assigning short tasks or chores), which allow for movement but are not discriminatory in nature.

Color-coding: Studies show that using color-coded systems can help kids with ADHD make better associations; they may also help with organizing and timekeeping. Encourage your child to color-code folders and notebooks for different classes or subjects. Later, when you write down assignments, you can keep the colors consistent by using similarly colored highlighters and pens (or fonts, if your daughter keeps a digital calendar or planner).

Assistive technology: Many schools offer technology-based educational tools to help children with ADHD manage their symptoms and co-occurring learning issues. Some common tools include transcription software, which allows a child to dictate ideas onto a computer document; audiobook library access; and C-Pens, which are pens that can highlight short pieces of text (such as homework) and read it aloud to a child. These are all tools that can help your child better access their education independently. Talk to your child's teacher to see if they might qualify for an assistive-technology evaluation.

Elementary School Signs and Challenges

In elementary school, as your daughter begins to learn to read and write, she may start to get flustered or frustrated by the added demands of homework assignments. You may notice that she resists starting homework, gets easily frustrated, or finds it difficult to initiate homework independently. In addition, she has to start organizing her backpack, keep track of her belongings, and also find time to make successful and lasting friendships.

Homework

In my work with parents of kids with ADHD, homework is quite possibly the most commonly discussed issue. Parents feel like they have to constantly nag their kids to get it done, and kids feel like their parents are not giving them a break. Many parents feel like they have tried everything and that nothing has worked to help sustain a successful system.

Here are some proven strategies to keep homework crises at bay:

- **Ask for assignments in advance.** Many teachers will give you all the assignments that are due Friday on Monday so that you can plan accordingly. If this is possible, encourage your daughter to sit down with you once a week and plan out her homework strategy. This can be extremely helpful for children who are busy with sports or activities so that they can maximize their time on less busy evenings or weekends.

- **Use a calendar and teach your daughter to consult it regularly.** Some people use a big dry-erase board for the whole family, and some have a calendar for each child. All of these systems can work, but what will work best for your child is the system that is realistic for your family. Google Calendar is a great digital option because you can combine calendars so that your daughter can see important events that you have, such as family holidays, parties, etc.

Socializing

Socializing for girls with ADHD is extremely important. Developing successful and positive peer relationships helps build their confidence, independence, and ability to relate to others.

- If your daughter is like Lexie, you may need to help her tone it down at times so that she doesn't turn off her peers with her "extra" behavior.

- For girls like Georgie, you may need to do some prodding or employ creative resourcefulness to help her find the right group of peers that can help bring her out of her shell.

- Girls like Kiara may need to build their confidence one-on-one as her natural tendency is to dominate in group settings.

At the elementary level, recess and lunchtime can be the most difficult moments for a child with ADHD. Those times tend to be the most unstructured and have the most overstimulating elements, such as noise, movement, and crowdedness. Finding ways to support your daughter in navigating these times can be hard because many schools have limited resources. Here are a few ideas to think about:

- **Ask if there are any lunchtime social skills groups or lunch bunches available.** Some schools offer these alternative lunchtime settings for children who may need extra support to work on their conversational skills or who benefit from practicing socializing in a smaller setting.

- **Find out what the rules are and what is allowed at both lunchtime and recess.** Sometimes schools will let your child bring a game, device, or toy that may help reduce physical impulsivity during highly stimulating times.

- **Request a shadow.** If your daughter repeatedly struggles, request that her teacher shadow or observe her during those times. It may be helpful to get an idea about what is triggering her so that some interventions can be put into place proactively.

Middle School Signs and Challenges

Middle school brings up a whole new set of challenges for parents and girls with ADHD alike. First, your daughter is starting to enter puberty, which means hormones are really influencing her moods and behavior. Next, your daughter's focus starts to shift toward her peer group. Your once close, cuddly girl may now want nothing to do with you and treat you like you have the plague when you ask for a hug.

School is her place of education, but it's also her place of socialization in addition to any activities in which she participates. She may start to deal with both girl and boy drama. Her dependence on her phone and social media may increase exponentially, bringing about a host of new worries for both of you. Finally, academic pressure increases. Teachers expect more independence and more responsibility, but your daughter may struggle to meet these demands.

Here are some tips for parents of middle school girls:

- **Request that all homework assignments be posted online as well as in the classroom.** This may help those who are less organized stay on top of all their assignments.

- **Get to know your daughter's guidance counselor.** This is someone who can help your daughter navigate her academic load as well as the increased responsibility expected by teachers.

- **Work with your daughter to create a weekly system of reviewing her upcoming assignments.** I often recommend this to parents of young adolescents. First, it's a great habit to start, and it can help a student begin to look at both long- and short-term assignments so that there are fewer surprises.

- **Encourage your daughter to speak to the school social worker or counselor if she is having any social issues.** This person can be a valuable resource and can help your daughter build some social problem-solving skills for when drama occurs during school hours and you aren't there to help.

- **Stay on top of your daughter's social media accounts.** Be aware of what she is posting and looking at and who she is communicating with.

As your daughter with ADHD enters puberty, you may notice some fairly common behavioral challenges. First, your daughter's focus will shift heavily to her social environment, so distraction may be at an all-time high, or she may struggle even more with organization or managing homework. Keep in mind that it's normal and she will still need your support, even though she prefers to be around her friends all the time. Moodiness may become the norm with your daughter. Simple requests from you that normally went unnoticed may be responded to with sarcasm, disrespect, or major attitude.

Socializing

You may remember that socializing becomes priority number one during adolescence. Your daughter may have previously told you every-thing that happened in her day, and now, she can barely answer you in one word. Remember that this is all normal developmentally. But you may worry about how impulsive behavior plays out when adolescents have access to cell phones, social media, and the Internet. Additionally, you may notice that everything becomes super dramatic: fights galore, gossip, backstabbing, and constant texting with friends.

How to Deal with Social Media

Social media adds an extra layer of complication for adolescent girls, as well as their parents. Not only do girls have to be conscious of their face-to-face interactions, but there is also an awareness of a constant conversation and commentary happening via text and social media apps (such as Instagram, Snapchat, and TikTok). Many parents have never dealt with social media before, and it can create several issues.

While some girls are able to separate themselves from what's happening online, others have a very difficult time with it. It's important to talk to your daughter openly as soon as she gets her first smartphone or device that allows her to communicate via text and social media. The important conversations should center around etiquette, dealing with online bullying, and sending and receiving pictures.

I once heard a parent ask a police officer, who was providing a parents' focused social media training, how old their child should be when they give them their first phone. He answered: When you feel comfortable with your child viewing pornography. This may sound harsh, but it is the reality. Once your child has access to texting, the Internet, and social media, they'll be able to find things they aren't ready to see. It's up to you to put in safeguards for them, whether it's apps to monitor their activity, limiting their time and access, or having periodic phone checks.

There is no way to completely safeguard your child from the dangers of online predators or bullying, but you can teach them how to handle themselves if they get into a tricky situation. A great resource is CommonSenseMedia.org.

Emerging Sexuality

During adolescence, your daughter may start to become boy (or girl) crazy and begin showing signs of her emerging sexuality. First crushes (and second . . . and third) may develop, and your daughter may start to show lots of interest and give lots of her attention to other boys or girls.

ADHD and Puberty

As your daughter starts to move into puberty, her brain will undergo many changes. Hormonally, the increase of estrogen can directly affect the levels of norepinephrine and dopamine in the brain. Due to this hormonal increase, it's not uncommon for a girl's ADHD symptoms to increase during puberty. This becomes especially apparent during menstruation, when hormonal levels are at their peak. You can help your daughter better prepare for these changes by helping her track her menstrual cycle.

Medications and ADHD

Many doctors recommend medications when treating ADHD. The decision to use medication to treat your daughter's ADHD is a very personal one. Some girls do great on medication, and others are fine without it. In this section, I will cover how ADHD medications treat ADHD symptoms and dispel some of the myths about using ADHD medications. I'll also go over the benefits and potential side effects of ADHD medications, and I'll explain the differences between stimulant-based and non-stimulant medications.

The Science of ADHD Medications

Stimulant-based medications, the most popular medications used to treat ADHD, are used for symptoms like lack of focus, hyperactivity, and difficulty sitting still. They work by increasing the release of certain chemicals in the brain, such as dopamine, which helps clear pathways in the brain so that it can communicate more effectively.

Facts vs. Myths

Myth: Medication will turn my child into a zombie.

Fact: The common medications used for ADHD are used to manage the symptoms of ADHD and generally don't have sedation qualities, so they shouldn't have significant effects on your child's overall demeanor or personality.

Myth: Once my child starts medication, they will form a dependence on it that they will never be able to break.

Fact: Some children need medication for short periods of time, and others use them over their lifetime. Every person is different.

Myth: Taking medication means my child is more likely to develop a substance-abuse problem.

Fact: Studies show that children with ADHD taking a prescribed stimulant are actually *less* likely to develop a substance-abuse problem. People who abuse stimulants are usually those without an ADHD diagnosis.

Benefits of ADHD Medications

According to CHADD, stimulant-based medications are considered to be some of the safest psychiatric medications available. Additionally, medication-based treatment is shown to be the most effective way to reduce the symptoms of ADHD, specifically impulsivity, distractibility, and hyperactivity. It's important to remember that stimulants aren't prescribed to control behavior but, instead, to manage the challenging symptoms that can prevent your child from having successful experiences both socially and academically.

Stimulants vs. Non-Stimulants

Studies show that stimulant-based medications have the best outcomes. A 1999 study by the MTA Cooperative Group found that 70 to 80 percent of children with ADHD who were prescribed a stimulant saw a reduction of symptoms. There are two main types of stimulant-based medications:

- Methylphenidate-based, such as Ritalin and Concerta

- Amphetamine-based, such as Adderall and Vyvanse

Within both of these families, there exist many different formulations. Short-acting stimulants are metabolized quickly, and extended-release (typically followed by ER or XR) stimulants stay active for upward of eight hours. In addition, medications come in different forms, such as a chewable, tablet, capsule, liquid, and patch. It's important that you discuss any of your concerns with your child's psychiatrist.

Non-stimulant medications are sometimes prescribed in children younger than six years old or when other co-occurring conditions are present, such as Tourette's syndrome. Strattera, clonidine, and guanfacine (Intuniv) are the most commonly prescribed. The research about the effectiveness of non-stimulant medication is less available because they haven't been studied as long.

Potential Side Effects

All drugs can have potential side effects. The most common side effects associated with stimulant-based medications are appetite loss, sleep disturbance, irritability, and, rarely, cardiac issues. Most doctors will order an EKG before prescribing a stimulant for your child if there is any family history of cardiac issues.

Non-stimulant medications carry potential side effects such as drowsiness, fatigue, and irritability. Additionally, Strattera is a medication that builds up in your child's bloodstream, so it can take up to six weeks to see the full efficacy of the medication.

Takeaways

I hope this chapter has helped you feel more confident managing the everyday issues that can arise. We've gone over how to handle tricky household transition times and how to best support your daughter at school, including elementary school challenges and the complications that come with middle school, hormones, and puberty. Finally, we discussed some of the pros and cons of medications so that you are armed with the correct information to make a decision about what is right for your daughter. Remember, there is no precise treatment protocol. The key things you can do as a parent are educate yourself about what is available and know your daughter the best that you can.

Now let's take a look at some of the common conditions that can occur alongside ADHD. We will get into building your daughter's self-esteem, how to spot the signs of anxiety and depression, and what to do if you think your daughter may have an eating disorder or is struggling with self-harm.

Chapter 3 Cheat Sheet:

- Sleep issues are common in kids with ADHD. Having a consistent, calming bedtime routine can be helpful.

- Work your way up to longer playdates to help develop social stamina in younger girls with ADHD.

- There are many different ways a child can be accommodated educationally at school either via an IEP or a Section 504 plan.

- In elementary school, communication with teachers is key to creating successful educational relationships for your daughter.

- Find out what socializing opportunities may be available if your daughter struggles socially.

- Middle school is a time of transition, but the added pressure of social media can make this time very complicated and fraught for parents.

- The decision to medicate is a personal/family decision. Read up on the available medication options. Talk to your doctor and do what is best for your child.

GIRLS WITH ADHD AND COEXISTING CONDITIONS

Having a daughter with ADHD means that you sometimes deal with other challenges, such as low self-esteem, depression, anxiety, eating disorders, and behavioral issues. An ADHD diagnosis doesn't mean that your daughter will necessarily have to deal with any of these issues, but it does increase the likelihood that she may deal with one or more of them. Knowing the warning signs and some of the symptoms can help you support your daughter early on and hopefully prevent these issues from becoming more serious. Let's cover all our bases and arm you with some helpful knowledge and new strategies.

Fostering Self-Esteem

Girls with ADHD are at risk of developing low self-esteem for a variety of reasons. One major reason is that they tend to internalize criticism more and may resort to self-critical thoughts and behaviors. Also, girls with ADHD may have less self-awareness about how it affects them, and they may not be able to identify problems as being associated with their ADHD. These risks may rise during the tween and adolescent years, when academic demands and the importance of peer acceptance increase. Some people believe that kids with ADHD are more susceptible to being sensitive to rejection. This means that they find rejection of any kind (criticism especially) to be really difficult to handle and will often ruminate.

Kiara

Kiara has been having a rough time with her friends lately. The main group she usually hangs out with has started to break into two groups, and there has been some conflict between them. Kiara feels slightly in the middle and doesn't know whom her allegiance should be with. Also, anytime anyone makes a slightly negative comment toward her, she feels really awful. She will go over and over it in her head and replay what she wishes she would have said. She also really takes these comments to heart.

Late Diagnosis Can Lead to Criticism

It's not uncommon for girls with ADHD to get diagnosed at a later age than boys. This may be for a variety of reasons. Some of the symptoms, such as hyperactivity and chattiness, may manifest differently in girls, and outdated gender perceptions may feed into this, too. There may be neurodevelopmental differences as well, since it is thought that the female brain may mature sooner than the male brain. Because girls get diagnosed later, this also means that they receive treatment later, and it's important to remember that a missed diagnosis can mean that your daughter's symptoms were labeled by others as laziness, silliness, or wild behavior instead of symptoms that were out of her control.

Girls Tend to Internalize

In addition to the complications that can arise with a late diagnosis, it's important to keep in mind that girls tend to internalize struggles or problems created by ADHD. Experts believe that girls with inattentive type ADHD (type 2) especially have a tendency to internalize feelings of rejection, loneliness, and low self-esteem. According to Dr. Ellen Littman, author of "The Secret Lives of Girls with ADHD," girls with inattentive ADHD resort to this form of coping the most. It may be because they often feel like outsiders among their peers, believe they are judged more harshly than others, and deal with their tendency to internalize by avoiding situations. While it may seem to their peers that these girls only care about themselves and want to be alone, girls with inattentive type ADHD are actually aware of their social short-comings, including the fact that they miss social cues, and may feel lonely and self-conscious.

Tips for Intervention

- **Model positive self-talk.** Find teaching moments throughout your day or week to model how to reframe negative or self-critical thoughts. For example, if you drop something, pay attention to what you say. Instead of "I'm so clumsy!" replace it with "I think I need to slow down and take a deep breath." When you hear your daughter making self-critical comments, ask her to reframe them. You can also create a positivity jar filled with self-affirming statements written down on slips of paper. Have your daughter take one out and read it when she is feeling frustrated or doubting her abilities.

- **Support your daughter in developing healthy friendships.** If your daughter has difficulty making or initiating friendships, have her practice conversation topics or openers with you. Reach out to her school and find out if there is a lunch bunch, social club, or extracurricular activity that she can join. Encourage your daughter to seek out friends that make her feel good about herself.

- **Help your daughter become more self-aware of her ADHD.** As girls become older, they become more self-conscious, but girls with ADHD struggle with the ability to self-reflect and become self-aware. Encouraging your daughter to identify her own ADHD symptoms will be an important step in helping her understand how it works. You can do this by supporting self-education. Have her read books on the subject, encourage her to talk to a professional who specializes in ADHD, or sit down with her and watch YouTube channels about ADHD. Make sure to ask open-ended questions after these activities to help her continue toward deeper self-awareness.

- **Have your daughter identify her strengths.** It's important for all girls to know what they are good at. Every child has strengths, and helping your child understand them and how to use them is very important. Remember that strengths can be character-based. For example, your daughter may be a great listener, fantastic leader, or patient teacher. Have a discussion with her about all the ways in which her strengths can help her and how they will continue to help her as she gets older.

- **Create a sticky-note success wall.** All girls need more positive messages. Girls with ADHD especially benefit from messages that promote feelings of self-worth. Start a wall or a poster board for your daughter, and every time she has a success or a positive moment, write it on a sticky note and display it. Make sure to note all kinds of successes (not just academic or athletic). Some examples are:

  » You made me smile today!

  » You worked SO hard on your cheer routine.

  » You made your friend feel better!

  » You gave a beautiful compliment.

  » You thought of someone else's needs.

Anxiety and Depression

A girl with ADHD means that her brain is constantly processing the world's information at different speeds, which may lead them to feel uneasy, nervous, or anxious. Additionally, children with ADHD have difficulty managing their emotions due to deficits in executive function skills, which may also lead to feelings of worry and sadness. Research shows that close to 30 percent of children with ADHD also have an anxiety disorder. Research also shows that children with ADHD receive more negative feedback than children without ADHD, which may also lead to feelings of guilt, shame, and worry. While all of this information may have you feeling uneasy or worried, the more you know, the better equipped you are to deal with any issues of anxiety or depression that may come up for your child. Also, when you first see the signs of anxiety or depression, make sure to reach out for help right away before symptoms worsen. Children are resilient and can make real positive strides and learn better coping techniques with some good professional support.

Signs of Anxiety

Anxiety can look slightly different in girls with ADHD than in girls without ADHD. Here are some key differences to note:

- You may notice changes in behavior, such as irritability, meltdowns, and bad moods that last longer than usual.

- Your daughter may worry or obsess about one thing in particular; for example, going to bed, the dark, an upcoming birthday party, or worrying about the future (such as a case of the what-ifs).

- Your daughter may start spending more time alone or isolate herself by watching TV or spending time on her iPad.

- Your daughter may display more disruptive or attention-seeking behaviors at school, such as goofing off, or she may have difficulty interacting with peers.

Tips for Intervention

- **Negative behaviors are your daughter's way of telling you that she is having difficulty coping with something.** Try not to immediately address the behavior; instead, ask her how she is feeling. If she can't tell you, ask her to draw how she is feeling, or encourage her to journal.

- **If your daughter is able to, talk to her about how she feels.** Practice listening to her and validating her feelings. Don't react, talk a lot, or try to give her advice. Validate her feelings by reflecting what she says back to her. For example, "I hear you say that school has been really hard for you lately. Can you tell me more about that?"

- **Urge your daughter to externalize or give her feelings an outlet.** A great way to do this is to encourage her to do something physical, like wall push-ups, going for a walk, or doing some jumping jacks.

- **Consider contacting a therapist if your daughter isn't feeling better.** A therapist who is trained in working with younger children will often have a background in play therapy.

Eating Disorders

While research is still limited on girls with ADHD and the prevalence of eating disorders, what is available does suggest that bulimia, binge eating, and obesity are more likely to develop in girls with ADHD. A 2009 study that appeared in the *International Journal of Eating Disorders* found that this is most likely due to issues with impulsivity and lack of self-control.

This list of signs to look for is by no means extensive. Remember, eating disorders present differently in each person. If you think your daughter has an eating disorder, it's always best to speak with a professional who is trained in eating disorders. For more information, check out the National Eating Disorders Association (NEDA).

What to Look For

- Changes in eating patterns, secretive eating, skipping meals, evidence of binge eating (wrappers, etc.), and/or hoarding food

- Significant weight gain or loss that may coincide with dressing differently

- Increased interest in the caloric value of different foods

- Increased interest in specific diets

- Feeling or acting uncomfortable around others at mealtimes

Tips for Intervention

- **Create a quiet, healthy space to talk.** Talk to your child if you suspect that changes in their eating habits or other signs are signaling a possible eating disorder. Remember that eating disorders can sometimes promote feelings of shame and guilt.

- **Address your concerns about your daughter's health and well-being.** Avoid topics like her appearance or her behaviors.

- **Don't condemn or judge any suspected behaviors.** Instead, focus on your concerns and what you have observed.

- **Offer support.** Give her some materials to read and agree to talk again about reaching out for more support in the form of a therapist.

- **Contact the National Eating Disorders Association (NationalEatingDisorders.org)** for more support or information.

- **Remember that the feelings of guilt and shame that are often associated with an eating disorder can lead to denial.** You may need to have several conversations or speak to a professional yourself to find out how to best assist your daughter.

Self-Harm

Girls—especially adolescent girls—with ADHD are more prone to engage in self-injurious behavior, according to an article that appeared in CHADD's *Attention* magazine. Non-suicidal self-injury (NSSI) refers to behaviors of self-harm without suicidal intent. These may include cutting, picking, or burning skin or a part of the body. In particular, girls with combined type ADHD (type 3) are more likely to be at risk for developing NSSI behaviors or even attempting suicide. It's important to remember that, according to the World Health Organization, suicide is the third leading cause of death in 15- to 19-year-olds.

Important

If you suspect your daughter is having thoughts of suicide or self-harm, seek immediate medical help and call the National Suicide Prevention Lifeline: 1-800-273-8255.

What to Look For

- Physical signs of self-harm, such as bruises, cuts, and abrasions; these may also get covered up by long-sleeve shirts or pants in an attempt to hide the scars.

- Tools used for self-harm, such as tweezers, nail clippers, scissors, knives, or other sharp instruments.

- Changes in behavior, such as socially withdrawing from family and friends, sleeping more or less, or changes in appetite.

Tips for Intervention

- **Try not to react with anger, guilt, or fear.** It's important to remember that young people who self-harm are already struggling with thoughts of shame and guilt, so reacting this way may backfire and cause your child to feel more alienated.

- **Normalize your child's feelings and discuss the importance of getting treatment.** Self-harming is a serious issue and should always be evaluated and treated by a qualified mental-health professional.

- **Find a qualified professional to help you and your child.** We will cover the different types of therapy in chapter 6.

Impulse Control

Impulsive behavior is probably one of the most frustrating and difficult things that parents of girls with ADHD have to deal with. You may wonder why your daughter is doing a certain behavior, which may be embarrassing, create very difficult situations for her socially, and impede her ability to engage appropriately with peers.

What to Look For

Girls with hyperactive-impulsive type ADHD (type 1) and combined type ADHD (type 3) are more likely to display behaviors that result from poor impulse control than girls with inattentive type ADHD (type 2). This may look like:

- Constant interrupting

- Difficulty keeping her hands to herself

- Inability to control the volume of her voice

- Excessive talking

- Lying

- Inability to keep personal distance

- Having very quick, intense social relationships with peers

Tips for Intervention

- **Choose the right physical activities.** If your daughter is younger and on the hyperactive-impulsive side, consider a full-sensory activity, such as swimming, gymnastics, or martial arts. Other sports, such as baseball and softball, may have too much downtime for an ADHD girl who needs stimulation.

- **Seek out a social skills group.** Some girls with ADHD really need a safe place to practice their social skills (such as learning how to keep a conversation going appropriately) and social problem-solving (such as how to handle disagreements). Groups led by a professional therapist can help your daughter practice these skills in a safe and controlled environment.

- **Play up your daughter's successes and praise her for making good choices.** Children with impulse-control issues get much more negative feedback, so play up the positive.

- **Use a "change the channel" approach for attention-seeking behavior.** Distract your child with a new activity. Moving to a new space or playing a song that they enjoy or find motivating may also prove helpful.

- **Help your daughter recognize the triggers that tend to set off impulsive behavior.** For example, some children have difficulty with birthday parties, holidays, and other highly anticipated events. Others may get more impulsive at certain times of the day or when they are around certain people or types of personalities. Helping your daughter know and understand her triggers can help you plan strategies and give her coping skills to better deal with them.

Peer Approval and Acceptance

Girls with ADHD may have a harder time receiving peer approval and acceptance and are more likely to get rejected socially at certain points throughout their development. Unfortunately, girls with ADHD need more positive peer interactions than they typically receive. Parents can help their daughters have better interactions by setting them up for success. Talk to their coach, teacher, or the instructor of their after-school and weekend activities and let them know about your daughter's strengths and weaknesses.

For example, you may know that your daughter responds well to certain language or catchphrases, or you may know that it's better for her coach to give her 10 minutes to cool off before addressing a tough situation.

Girls with ADHD and Gender Expectations

There are not many studies out yet about how gender roles may affect the development of girls with ADHD, but from what we do know, it's safe to say that girls and nonbinary children may not get the same attention in terms of early diagnostics, interventions, and services that boys do.

Empowering Girls with ADHD to Use Their Voice

Because we know that girls tend to get diagnosed later and also tend to internalize the symptoms or problems that ADHD causes them, it's important to teach your daughter how to self-advocate. Speak to her regularly about the importance of asking for help to normalize for her that there is no shame in needing assistance at school, in sports, or with friends.

Georgie

Georgie has started hanging out with a new group of girls that she met in her Thursday afternoon drawing class. They go to a different school than her, but she has enjoyed getting to know them. Recently, they have started goofing off and being rude to their drawing instructor, whom Georgie adores. Georgie doesn't know how to maintain a friendship with them while also letting them know that she doesn't think their behavior toward their teacher isn't right. She doesn't feel ready to confront them as a group. After discussing the dilemma with her mother, she decides to speak to each girl individually about it. It turns out, none of the girls really enjoy showing off in front of their teacher, but they were going along with the instigator. They all agree to not join in the next time it happens. Georgie feels much better about standing up for herself and is looking forward to the next class.

Takeaways

In this chapter, we have covered some of the conditions that can coexist in girls with ADHD, including anxiety, depression, eating disorders, impulsive behavior, and self-harming. You should have a better sense of what to look for, as well as have some helpful interventions to use if you are concerned about your daughter. In chapter 5, we will get into how ADHD affects your daughter on a daily basis by learning more about executive function skills and how to address deficits in them. I'll teach you some helpful strategies to encourage your daughter to start building and strengthening all of her executive function skills.

Chapter 4 Cheat Sheet:

- Finding ways to foster self-esteem is important for girls with ADHD because they tend to internalize more.

- Support your daughter's self-esteem by modeling and helping her develop healthy friendships.

- Know the signs of anxiety and depression, such as major changes in behavior and mood.

- Seek out the right activities and support to reduce negative experiences, such as impulsive behavior, and increase successful interactions.

PART THREE: **THRIVING WITH ADHD**

CHAPTER 5

BUILDING LIFE SKILLS

I n this chapter, we are going to get into the ways in which executive function–skill deficits affect girls with ADHD and how you can help your daughter strengthen them. We'll discuss time management, problem-solving, motivation, self-discipline, and emotional regulation. I am going to give you some hands-on strategies to get your daughter on track with her schedule and organization and to start improving her focus and concentration.

Executive Function Skills

As we discussed in chapter 2 (see page 28), executive function skills are the brain's ability to organize, access information, and regulate emotions.

All people with ADHD will have deficits in some or all of their executive function skills. Luckily, there are ways to strengthen them (more on that later), but let's go over each of the skills and the ways in which they play out in girls with ADHD.

Time Management

Girls with ADHD have difficulty with temporal awareness or their sense of time. For this reason, five minutes may pass, and it could seem like an eternity (especially if they are doing something they dislike). Alternatively, when they are doing something they love or find stimulating, they may completely lose track of time, which can cause issues of lateness or impact her ability to manage and adhere to a schedule. Girls with ADHD may also have difficulty estimating how long a particular task will take, which can lead to late nights of doing homework and working on projects.

Lexie

When it comes to time management, the struggle is real for Lexie. It drives her parents crazy that she doesn't ever seem to be aware of the clock or feel driven by time or deadlines. She is always rushing to get out of the house on time, and she always thinks she has way more time to get things done than she does. It's even starting to impact her social life. She is late to meet friends when she says she will or makes time-sensitive promises she can't keep (e.g., promising to text her best friend in 10 minutes, and then completely forgetting).

Planning and Prioritizing

The ability to plan and prioritize affects girls with ADHD, especially as they move into the adolescent and teen years. Academically, they may have difficulty with a large assignment—such as a research paper—and breaking it down into smaller, manageable tasks. Additionally, when confronted with a list of tasks, they may struggle with figuring out how to prioritize which task should get done first (such as homework assignments).

Kiara

Kiara has a hard time when it comes to planning and prioritizing. She often struggles during weeks that she has competitions and multiple assignments. She gets overwhelmed seeing everything that she has to accomplish. She will often choose to work on the least time-sensitive project rather than prioritizing tasks based on deadlines and what's coming up. She has a hard time seeing and recognizing this as an issue until after it starts to impact her negatively, and she also struggles to ask for help. Recently, Kiara has started putting all of her assignments on Google Calendar. She color-codes her assignments and adds frequent reminders for when certain assignments should be started and finished. This seems to be helping.

Organizing

It's very common for girls with ADHD to struggle with organization. For example, your daughter's backpack may always be a mess of papers. She may never be able to find her phone or keys because her room is cluttered, and she may have little or no idea how to develop systems or ways to organize her belongings. Girls with ADHD often lack the innate ability to group similar items together or create systems that help keep things or information in one place.

Georgie

Georgie has the most difficult time with staying organized. Her room, her backpack, her locker—they're all a jumbled mess of papers, folders, and notebooks. Papers are the worst. She's always losing her homework assignments and important papers, which causes a lot of stress and anxiety for her. Georgie would like to be more organized, but her brain just doesn't naturally think that way.

Task Initiation

Have you ever watched your daughter struggle with starting a task, such as a homework assignment, a chore, or even something she enjoys doing, like an art project? Initiating tasks is an executive function skill that often gets mislabeled as "laziness." The ability to self-motivate to start an activity is often affected by some of the other executive function skills—for example, being organized enough to have the tools you need to be ready for the task.

Working Memory

Your brain has three different types of memory: short-term memory, long-term memory, and working memory. Short-term memory consists of information that doesn't get stored (shopping lists and homework assignments from three days ago). Long-term memory is information that is stored and can be accessed later, such as phone numbers, addresses, birthdays, etc. Working memory is the ability to manipulate short- and long-term memory. It can help your daughter remember and carry out instructions, do mental math, and problem-solve. Working memory can be thought of as your brain's internal sticky-note system, where you can store information to access when you need it. For people with ADHD, the sticky notes aren't available, or they get erased or lost, and they lose the information needed to complete the process at hand.

Emotional Regulation

The ability to regulate emotions reasonably is an executive function skill that plays out more in relationships, especially with peers and socializing. Deficits in emotional regulation look like meltdowns in younger girls with ADHD or excessively aggressive/emotional/angry outbursts in older children. These outbursts may not match the size of the problem at hand as well.

Thinking Flexibly

Being able to think flexibly is also a skill that affects many girls with ADHD. You may notice that your daughter has a one-track mind when it comes to certain topics, ideas, or expectations. Or she may have a very difficult time shifting gears if plans or schedules change or if something does not go her way.

Self-Monitoring and Self-Reflection

Self-monitoring and self-reflection are important executive function skills because they help create self-awareness that can allow your daughter to make adjustments. Deficits in this skill can be frustrating for parents because it can be incredibly difficult to watch your daughter make the same mistake over and over again (whether it's social, academic, or otherwise).

Helping Girls Develop Executive Function Skills

Now let's help your ADHD daughter start flexing some of those executive function–skill muscles. I'm going to teach you some of my top tips and tricks to help build stronger skills.

Building Working Memory

Working memory can be strengthened by playing games with younger children that use visual memory (such as matching games) or seek-and-find games (such as *Where's Waldo* or *I Spy*). Older girls can try an app, such as Lumosity or Elevate. These can be great reorganizing activities; think of them like pressing the reset button or rebooting your computer. But when using these games or skills, use them for no more than five minutes.

Encourage your daughter to do less multitasking and focus on one task at a time. Have her use checklists for specific routines and keep them visually displayed in key areas (bathroom, bedroom, kitchen, etc.). It's also a good idea to help her create routines for certain times of the day. When a routine is consistently practiced at the same time of day, it greatly increases the likelihood for successful repetition.

Developing Determination to Finish Tasks

You can help reduce the instances in which your daughter starts many projects and activities but never finishes them by having her set an intention for every task she begins. Ask her to visualize what she would like to accomplish. For older girls, have them write down their goal and put it on a sticky note fastened somewhere it cannot be missed.

Another way to reduce the anxiety related to finishing a task is to help your daughter break down larger tasks into mini tasks. For example, if she has a book report due in a month, sit down with her and break the task into eight mini tasks (aim for two tasks per week). You can make notecards that outline each task (e.g., choose a book, read/finish the book, write an outline, write the introduction, etc.).

Developing Emotional Regulation and Flexible Thinking

Encourage your daughter to start engaging in some type of mindfulness activity. She can try a yoga class, follow a meditation video on YouTube, listen to a meditation podcast, or even take a short walk in nature. Mindfulness is also a great way to help the ADHD brain slow down, and it can help increase frustration tolerance for those who struggle with lower levels.

Another great strategy is to help your daughter practice delayed reaction when she is feeling a strong feeling. This can help reduce impulsive reactions that can cause hurt feelings in others and, later on, feelings of shame and guilt in herself. Encourage your daughter to set a timer or take a walk before she responds to an upsetting text message or an instigation from a sibling.

Creating Time Management Systems

Girls with ADHD may sense time differently than those without ADHD. Have your daughter experiment with different ways of measuring time to help her experience it better. For example, if you want your daughter to take a five-minute shower, play a five-minute song and tell her that when the song is over, the shower should be over.

Other ideas include using a visual timer, such as an hourglass, or one of the various visual timer apps available on phones. You can also help your daughter learn to estimate how long tasks will take her by helping her create a schedule for things like homework, playdates, etc.

Finally, kids with ADHD are notoriously bad at time estimation, so practicing this skill will be an important routine. Start by asking your daughter to estimate things that she does regularly (such as making her bed, brushing her teeth, etc.), then transition to things that are harder to estimate (reading a chapter in a book).

Reducing Forgetfulness

List writing is one of the key processes that girls with ADHD should be encouraged to adopt as a habit. Show your daughter how to make a daily list of things that she needs to do. You can have her keep lists on her phone (if she's older), a sticky note, or a bullet journal if she prefers to be more artistic with her lists and enjoys flexing her creative muscles (check out Pinterest for examples).

You can also teach your daughter how to do a brain dump list before she goes to bed, writing down anything that she doesn't want to forget for the next day. A great way to encourage this behavior in your daughter is to sit down and make a list yourself at the end of the night. Perhaps you and your daughter can sit down and make your lists together.

Modeling Organization

Help your daughter stay organized by modeling organization for her. Be mindful of how you keep your spaces and environment and model organization as much as possible. Assist her with creating systems in her room and places in which she likes to hang out that will help her find her belongings—for example, using a color-coding system for school subjects.

You can also split her room (or other personal space) into zones. For example, she can have a relaxation zone (where she keeps a chair, items related to hobbies, etc.), a work zone near her desk (where she can keep her school things), and a sleep zone (where her bed is).

Learning to Plan

Show your daughter how to use a calendar at an early age. Have a calendar visually displayed for younger girls either in their bedroom or in a high-traffic area where they can access it daily. Go over the calendar with your daughter and try to start a weekly habit of looking at the week and month ahead of time so that she can be prepared for upcoming events and make adjustments in her schedule.

The Gifts of ADHD

All girls with ADHD have amazing gifts. One special trait of girls with ADHD is that most learn how to create their own coping skills or strategies to deal with weaknesses or difficult moments. Learn to think of your daughter's strengths as small muscles that need to be flexed frequently so that they can grow. And try to keep in mind that personality traits that adults deem "difficult" in children can flourish into amazing talents.

The girl who is "stubborn" may have incredible persistence in her career.

The girl who is "highly emotional and sensitive" may become emotionally intuitive.

The girl who is "bossy" may make an incredible leader.

The girl who is "impulsive" may become creative and innovative as an adult.

What is your daughter's special trait? How can you foster it to become a superpower? How can you change the way you view it to allow it to become a positive instead of a negative?

Takeaways

In this chapter, we've discussed what executive function skills are and how deficits in them may appear in your daughter with ADHD. I've taught you some new strategies that can help strengthen your daughter's executive function skills and start building some new habits and coping skills. In the following chapter, we will tackle some practical tips for success for girls with ADHD, as well as different types of therapy that may be helpful along your journey.

CHAPTER 6

TIPS FOR SUCCESS

I n this last chapter, we are going to talk about how to support your daughter with the best health routines for eating, exercise, sleep, and managing stress. From time to time, you and your daughter may need some professional support, so I will also discuss the different types of therapy that can be helpful for girls with ADHD and their family members. Finally, I'll touch on how to create a dynamic support team for your awesome girl.

Living to Succeed

Creating healthy routines for everyday behaviors, such as sleeping and eating, can be incredibly helpful for girls with ADHD. Many children with ADHD struggle with maintaining regular healthy habits, especially for sleeping. There are a few strategies to keep in mind that may help instill a sense of calm and relaxation that will be conducive for sleep.

Sleep

In my work with children with ADHD, issues with sleep are probably among the most common problems I hear about from parents. Additionally, sleep trouble can be one of the most difficult problems to deal with because of how it can impact family stress levels. After all, if your child isn't sleeping well, you most likely aren't sleeping well, either.

According to the National Sleep Foundation, a recent study showed that 50 percent of children with ADHD showed signs of sleep-disordered breathing. A 2006 study in *SLEEP*, the official journal of the Sleep Research Society, showed that children with ADHD displayed higher rates of daytime sleepiness than children without ADHD. Additionally, a 2006 study out of the Adler Center for Research in Child Development and Psychopathology found that restless leg syndrome has also been linked to children with ADHD. There are a few ways to create the best sleep environment and set your daughter up for sleep success.

- **Try to aim for the same bedtime every night.** Having a regular bedtime sets the stage for a healthy routine, and it also ensures that your daughter will hopefully begin to get sleepy around the same time every evening.

- **Have a calm bedtime routine and try to stick to the same order.** Following the same routine every night, such as showering, reading, and listening to calming music, starts to send signals to your daughter's brain that it's time to get ready to sleep.

- **Limit digital and screen time at least 30 minutes to an hour before bed.** Studies show that the light from screens actually sends signals to your daughter's brain to stay awake, so limiting screen time isn't a punishment—it's a healthy habit.

- **Consult with a neurologist or a sleep specialist.** If your daughter is consistently waking up or doesn't get a healthy amount of sleep for her age, a specialist may suggest doing a sleep study to rule out sleep apnea or other sleep disorders that can interrupt her sleep behaviors.

Exercise

Exercise is important for all children, but children with ADHD especially need the physical release of energy (especially those with hyperactive-impulsive type ADHD). A 2014 study published in the

Journal of Abnormal Child Psychology found that exercise helps increase blood flow to the brain, which boosts neurotransmitters and can help with impulsiveness, attention, and planning. For younger children, try swimming, skating, and diving, which require full-body involvement and are stimulating to their senses. Other sports, such as martial arts, dancing, rock climbing, and gymnastics, are great choices as well. If your child isn't into organized sports, encourage some time outdoors in nature by going to a local park or taking a family hike. All of these activities can help reduce stress and instill a sense of calm and well-being, as well as help with sleep.

Nutrition

It's probably not a surprise that nutrition is a key component to raising a healthy girl with ADHD. Ensuring that your daughter eats a well-balanced diet is important, but there are other things to keep in mind, especially for girls with ADHD. Consider adding in more carbohydrates with a low-glycemic index, such as whole grains, grapes, apples, cherries, berries, and grapefruit. These foods help power the brain by releasing a steady supply of sugar into the body to help your daughter's brain stay better regulated. Additionally, a protein-rich diet will help fuel the chemicals in your daughter's brain. Protein helps create amino acids, which help make neurotransmitters. Fueling the neurotransmitters in your daughter's brain sets her up for success. Consider ways to boost her protein intake, especially at breakfast, by adding in eggs, whey protein, Greek yogurt, and lean animal proteins (such as chicken).

Supplements

If your daughter is a picky eater (like mine!) or it's hard to get her to eat fruits and vegetables, you may want to consider adding in some supplements to ensure that she is getting the best nutrition to support her brain. There are a few supplements supported by research that can help. First, omega-3 fatty acids (which usually come in the form of fish oil) are the most researched supplement when it comes to ADHD. Several studies cited in a June 2019 article of *ADDitude* magazine support the proposition that the regular use of this supplement can be helpful for attention, impulsivity, and hyperactivity.

Stress Management

Let's face it: ADHD can sometimes make life feel a little out of control. This feeling can lead to stress. It's important to model stress management techniques for your daughter to help her learn them for herself and begin to incorporate them as coping tools. Here are a few ways:

- **Take deep breaths.** Sit down with your daughter and practice abdominal breathing together (breathe in through your nose and out through your mouth), imagining that you are filling your abdomen with air and letting it out.

- **Play!** Playing with your daughter is one of the best ways to encourage stress relief. For younger children, play is their first language; it's how they express themselves and process the world. Sit down on the floor with your daughter and spend 10 minutes drawing, building, or playing a board game.

- **Help your daughter create a stress or worry box.** Fill it with items that help her feel better, such as modeling clay, a stress ball, a journal, and headphones to listen to music.

Therapy and ADHD

At some point in your journey, it may be helpful for you to consult with a professional to get some insight, learn some new strategies, or to just have a sounding board. Let's briefly go into some of the types of therapy that may be helpful.

Family Therapy

Family therapy focuses on examining family dynamics to try to strengthen communication and minimize conflict. It's a great place to start if your children cannot peacefully coexist in the same room or if it feels like dominant personalities in the family make it harder for others to be heard.

In family therapy, you may learn and practice skills as a family, such as listening techniques, reflective listening, and de-escalation skills to defuse tense family moments.

Cognitive Behavioral Therapy

Cognitive behavioral therapy (CBT) is one of the most popular types of therapy available. It's based on the idea that negative thinking patterns can lead to negative emotions and moods, such as anxiety or depression. CBT tends to give the therapist a more active role, teaching the client ways to redirect or challenge negative patterns. There is more responsibility on the client to engage and sometimes complete work outside of the therapy session. CBT has become very popular with children with ADHD because of the behavioral component and because the research supports its success.

Mindfulness-Based Cognitive Therapy

Mindfulness-based cognitive therapy (MBCT) combines the ideas of cognitive therapy with meditative practices, such as meditation and breathing exercises. Incorporating mindfulness and meditation into your daughter's routine can be extremely helpful. She can learn how to clear her mind when she feels flooded with competing thoughts or worries. She can also practice mindfulness on her own by taking a meditation class at a local yoga studio, or she can try it at home by using an app, such as Headspace or Calm.

You know that saying, "It takes a village to raise a child"? Well, in many ways, it's true. We are lucky this day and age to have access to more professionals who are aware of the needs of an ADHD child.

Here are some professionals to consider adding to your daughter's team:

- **Therapist**: A person with whom your daughter can vent, learn new coping skills, and gain new insights so that she can better self-reflect.

- **Tutor**: A tutor can be especially helpful as kids move into middle and high school, when academic demands increase (and compete with social needs). A good tutor can reinforce learned material and work with your daughter to break down concepts.

- **ADHD coach**: In addition, an ADHD coach can also work with your child on organization skills and executive function skills.

Parental Care

Taking care of yourself is an important aspect of helping your daughter succeed. Let's discuss how you can be your best self so that you can show your daughter how she can be her best self.

We all have moments of burnout when we reach our limits, lose our patience, and feel unprepared. However, accessing your inner peace and using your reserves of calm are going to help you model for your daughter how to deal with high-stress situations. Here are a few tips that I've learned in working with parents, as well as ones that I use myself:

Exercise: Adopting some sort of consistent exercise practice can do wonders for your stress level. Having a physical outlet for stress will alleviate pent-up energy and create space for patience and kindness. Mindfulness practices like yoga are great, but other forms of exercise like gardening, walking the dog, or taking a group fitness class are also great choices. My go-to is to get my exercise done early in the morning before anyone else is awake. I think of it as my special alone time that's just for me.

Friendship/camaraderie: Having a source of encouragement, such as friends who know what you are going through or a parenting support group, can be a great way to burn off steam. We all need to laugh, talk, listen, and connect with those who understand us.

Hobbies: Having an interest outside of your job, your role as a parent, and your children can be a great way to release stress and connect to your brain's pleasure center. Music, writing, art, cooking, crafts, gardening, and volunteering are great ways to spend some time away from the thoughts that often crowd and congest our minds as parents. Even if you don't have a hobby, trying something new can be a great way to distract yourself. There are loads of things you can do to start a new hobby: order a craft kit online, watch a "How to Knit" video on YouTube, or take a language class online.

How ADHD Affects Parents

Having a daughter with ADHD can challenge your image of yourself as a parent. You may feel less confident and start to question your abilities or effectiveness. It's important to remember that it's normal to feel unsure, particularly if you previously felt confident in your parenting style. Keep in mind that different children do well with different parenting styles. Just as your daughter may need to learn new tricks and strategies to help balance herself out, you may also need to adjust your expectations and learn some new ways of thinking about parenting. Think about it like this: If you got a new promotion at work that required learning some new skills, you wouldn't expect to be immediately successful. It would take time, patience, and diligence, right? Be patient with yourself; you are learning a new way to relate to your child. By doing so, you are helping her become the best version of herself.

Care for the Caretaker

Everyone gets burned out from time to time, but caretakers especially bear the burden of constantly thinking about others before themselves. This can lead to you feeling exhausted, drained, and having diminished patience levels both with yourself and your family. It's important to remember that if you want to be the best parent you can be, you have to make yourself a priority as well. Practice daily self-care by getting enough exercise, sleep, and time to do what you enjoy. By doing this, you are also modeling good, healthy habits for your daughter and showing her that taking care of herself is an important part of her self-care routine.

Parenting Skills Training

We can all brush up on our parenting skill sets once in a while. We are all constantly evolving, so what may have been useful and effective for your daughter at age seven may change completely when she is 12. Getting professional advice via reading parenting books or even seeing a therapist can be extremely useful. I always tell the parents I work with that I only recommend one parenting book. In all my years working with children and teens with ADHD, I have found Dr. Ross W. Greene's *The Explosive Child* to be the most revolutionary book to influence the field of parenting. Remember, if you are considering meeting with a therapist to brush up on your parenting skills, this is not an admission of weakness or defeat. It's quite the opposite; it's a willingness to discover new perspectives and consider new ideas.

Tips on Being More Mindful

Mindfulness is defined as bringing one's awareness to the present. In our busy, global, digital worlds, it can be extremely challenging to bring this concept into parenting. As parents, we have to juggle jobs, homes, and marriages/relationships, so you may have to balance the time you spend with your daughter with all of these responsibilities. Incorporating some of the principles of mindfulness into your parenting can help reduce family stress levels and conflicts. Here are some ideas to keep in mind:

- **No judging.** Become aware of how judgments influence your thinking. Don't try to control or stop it when you notice these thoughts happening, but bring your awareness to them.

- **Trust your own ideas and thoughts.** It can be hard to feel confident when you begin opening your mind, but allow yourself to think freely.

- **See the world through a beginner's mind.** Think of how your child saw the world as a preschooler, finding wonder and joy in life's tiny details. It's okay to not have all the answers.

Mindfulness Exercise: Go to Your Happy Place

This is a great mindfulness exercise to use when you are feeling frazzled, stressed, stretched, or just plain burned out. Remember that your mind can be your worst enemy: If you are thinking negatively, you will start to feel negatively, which can leave you feeling anxious, down, or depressed. The opposite can be true as well: If you can get your mindset back to a healthier place, you will feel more effective as a parent and less trapped in your parenting style. (Pro tip: Once you've mastered this exercise for yourself, use it and teach it to your daughter. Model mindfulness and make it contagious!)

First, close your eyes and take several deep breaths in through your nose and out through your mouth. Observe the difference that taking a few deep breaths has on your body. Think of a place (real or imagined) that brings you a sense of peace and calm. It can be a place you went on vacation (like a beach) or a room in your home. Make sure it's a place that you only associate with good, positive feelings. Picture yourself in this place. If it's a beach, try playing the sounds of waves crashing. Allow yourself to hear the sounds, smell the smells, and really experience the place of relaxation with your senses. If other thoughts enter your head, just observe them as if you were watching a teleprompter: Observe them as they arrive, and observe them as they leave. Don't try to control them. Spend a few minutes in your happy place, taking note of how visiting this place in your mind makes you feel. When you're finished, take those happy feelings back with you. Remind yourself that you can visit this place whenever you like.

Inclusive Treatment Plan and ADHD

Your daughter is a complex being with many working parts. In order to keep her healthy and at her best, you'll need to build a team of support around her. Think of it like her safety net (as well as yours) for difficult times and her cheerleading squad for the moments of celebration and solidarity. Here are some of the key people to loop into your daughter's treatment plan.

Parents

I always tell parents I work with to find a support group. By this, I mean surround yourself with people who love, understand, and support you as a family and love your daughter. When it comes to other parents, your daughter will look to many adult influences in her life, and the other parents (such as parents of friends) will play an important part in this.

Sometimes you'll have to seek out the parents of other children with ADHD. Facebook has a ton of groups for parents who are raising children with ADHD. You can also reach out to your local associations. In my state of New Jersey, we have statewide parent advocacy networks known as Special Education Parent Advisory Groups (SEPAG), which can be a great source of information and support. I am a member of my local chapter, which distributes information and resources on a local level.

It can also be helpful to find a parenting support group run by a therapist or parent. This can be a source of information and support and a great place to vent, get ideas, and learn new information.

Teachers

As we've already discussed, developing a good teamwork approach with your daughter's teachers is important to ensuring her success at school. I know that this isn't always easy, but, especially when it isn't, try to find a common ground or a place of understanding.

The truth is that some teachers are great about understanding and adapting to the needs of a student with ADHD, and some aren't. But if a teacher isn't initially great about accommodating your daughter's learning needs, that doesn't mean that they can't become better with the right communication and information. Cultivating these relationships alongside your daughter shows her the importance of working on a relationship.

Here are some great questions to ask your daughter's teacher, which can help start a dialogue:

1. How do you see ADHD affecting my daughter in your classroom?

2. What challenges in the classroom can be supported or strengthened at home?

3. How can we communicate better with you?

4. What would be helpful for you to know about my daughter's learning challenges and strengths?

5. What do you see as my daughter's learning challenges and strengths?

Therapists

As a therapist, I always tell the parents that I work with that their relationship with me is equally as important as their child's. I tell them that they are their daughter's 24-hour therapist—they provide support, love, and understanding to their daughter when she needs it. If you are working with a therapist, make sure that the lines of communication are open and clear.

Doctors

Finding a doctor who understands ADHD and all its complexities can be hard. Luckily, most professionals are more versed in information about ADHD these days. It's important to find a doctor who views your daughter as more than just a diagnosis: She's a human being with a full spectrum of emotions and talents.

A Plan of Action

Now that we've reached the conclusion of this book, I hope you feel more confident as a parent who can support your daughter to flourish and thrive. A diagnosis of ADHD is not a life sentence. It's a badge that your daughter will wear—one that takes courage and will build her character.

We are lucky to live in a time that is recognizing the differences that gender can have on certain diagnoses. As science and research catch up to things we already know about girls with ADHD, we will learn more about their unique differences. Perhaps more important, we will also learn about their strengths, resilience, and gifts.

Remember that when you feel shaky as a parent, it's just because you want to do your best. Reach out to your support system and continue to build a healthy safety net for your daughter. There will always be ups and downs, but you are blessed with a unique daughter who is going to grow into her talents and skills. With her gifts, she is going to do great things.

RESOURCES

BOOKS

Raising Human Beings: Creating a Collaborative Partnership with Your Child by Ross W. Greene, PhD: Another wonderful resource by Dr. Greene about how parenting differently can lead to more positive outcomes.

The Explosive Child: A New Approach for Understanding and Parenting Easily Frustrated, Chronically Inflexible Children by Ross W. Greene, PhD: This is the only parenting book I recommend to parents. Dr. Greene has revolutionized the way that negative behaviors are viewed and addressed by parents and professionals.

The Out-of-Sync Child: Recognizing and Coping with Sensory Processing Disorder by Carol Stock Kranowitz: A great read if you feel like your child has any sensory issues.

Understanding Girls with ADHD: How They Feel and Why They Do What They Do by Kathleen Nadeau, Ellen Littman, and Patricia Quinn: A wonderful wealth of information by the leading women experts on ADHD.

WEBSITES

ADDitudeMag.com (check out the free parenting webinars!): *ADDitude* magazine is the publication written for parents of children with ADHD, as well as adults with ADHD.

CHADD.org: The website for Children and Adults with Attention-Deficit/Hyperactivity Disorder. A great place to start reading. Tons of resources, plus all the latest research.

KaleidoscopeSociety.com: A community of women with ADHD who seek to empower others as well as raise understanding and awareness.

LivesInTheBalance.org: This website encompasses all of Ross Greene's resources.

SmartGirlsWithADHD.com: A blog geared toward empowering girls and women with ADHD.

TheNSF.org: The website for the National Sleep Foundation. A great abundance of knowledge about anything related to sleep, as well as advice on good sleep habits, information on sleep disorders, research, etc.

PODCASTS

Distraction with Dr. Ned Hallowell: A podcast hosted by one of the thought leaders in the ADHD realm that examines topics that intersect with ADHD in our current climate.

Parenting Your Challenging Child by Ross W. Greene, PhD: A podcast led by Ross Greene and a parent who has gone through his Collaborative Problem Solving (CPS) training. It addresses parents' questions and issues using the CPS model.

PARENTING SUPPORT

ADDitude—ADHD Support Group: This Facebook group for those with ADHD offers positive connection and support without judgment or criticism. Facebook.com/groups/additudemag.

CHADD Parent to Parent Training: Run by CHADD, this online training program provides support and information from other parents of children with ADHD. The introductory course is free.

TED TALK

"This Is What It's Really Like to Live with ADHD" by Jessica McCabe: An honest account of what it's truly like to live with ADHD.

YOUTUBE CHANNEL

"How to ADHD" by Jessica McCabe: A channel geared toward informing, understanding, and giving practical advice.

FOR GIRLS

Books

Attention, Girls!: A Guide to Learn All about Your ADHD by Patricia Quinn: Written by one of the leading minds in the field of women with ADHD, this book is geared toward tweens and offers practical strategies and advice.

The Girls' Guide to AD/HD: Don't Lose This Book! by Beth Walker: Written in a light, conversational tone, this book discusses how ADHD manifests in girls as well as other related issues.

Thriving with ADHD Workbook for Teens: Improve Focus, Get Organized, and Succeed by Allison Tyler, LCSW: This workbook aims to help teens identify weaknesses in executive function skills and learn new habits and tricks to strengthen them.

Websites

CHADD: Women and Girls: CHADD.org/for-adults/women-and-girls

"Stop the Cycle of Shame for Girls with ADHD" by Katherine Ellison: ADDitudeMag.com/adhd-in-girls-shame.

ADHD Support Group

ADDitude—ADHD Support Group: This Facebook group for those with ADHD offers positive connection and support without judgment or criticism. Facebook.com/groups/additudemag.

REFERENCES

"ADHD and Anxiety: What You Need to Know." Understood. Accessed December 2019. Understood.org/en/learning-thinking-differences /child-learning-disabilities/add-adhd/adhd -and-anxiety-what-you -need-to-know.

"ADHD and Coexisting Disorders." National Resource Center on ADHD. Accessed November 2020. CHADD.org/wp-content/uploads/2018/04 /coexisting.pdf.

ADHD Editorial Board. "Change Your Diet, Find Your Focus." *ADDitude* magazine. Last modified October 5, 2020. ADDitudeMag .com/can-the-right-diet-ease-add-symptoms.

ADHD Editorial Board. "The Most Common Myths about ADHD—Busted!" *ADDitude* magazine. Last modified June 27, 2019. ADDitudeMag.com/myths-about-adhd.

Bauermeister, José J., et al. "ADHD and Gender: Are Risks and Sequela of ADHD the Same for Boys and Girls?" *The Journal of Child Psychology and Psychiatry* 48, no. 8 (August 2007): 831-9. doi.org/10.1111/j.1469-7610.2007.01750.x.

"Hormones and Women's ADHD Symptoms—Part Two." CHADD, ADHD Weekly. Accessed November 2019. CHADD.org/adhd-weekly /hormones-and-womens-adhd-symptoms-part-two.

Chalker, Samantha A. "ADHD, Self-Harm, and Suicide." CHADD, *Attention* magazine, Summer 2017. CHADD.org/attention-article /adhd-self-harm-and-suicide.

Cortese, Samuele, et al. "Sleep in Children with Attention-Deficit/ Hyperactivity Disorder: Meta-Analysis of Subjective and Objective Studies." *Journal of the American Academy of Child & Adolescent*

Psychiatry 48, no. 9 (September 2009): 894-908. doi.org/10.1097/CHI.0b013e3181ac09c9.

Danielson, Melissa L., et al. "Prevalence of Parent-Reported ADHD Diagnosis and Associated Treatment among US Children and Adolescents, 2016." *Journal of Clinical Child & Adolescent Psychology* 47, no. 2 (January 2018): 199-212. doi.org/10.1080/15374416.2017.1417860.

Golan, Natali, Eli Shahar, Sarit Ravid, and Giora Pillar. "Sleep Disorders and Daytime Sleepiness in Children with Attention-Deficit/Hyperactive Disorder." *SLEEP* 27, no. 2 (March 2004): 261-266. doi.org/10.1093/sleep/27.2.261.

Grilo, Carlos M., Marney A. White, and Robin M. Masheb. "DSM-IV Psychiatric Disorder Comorbidity and Its Correlates in Binge Eating Disorder." *International Journal of Eating Disorders* 42, no. 3 (April 2009): 228-34. doi.org/10.1002/eat.20599.

Hirsch, Glenn S. "Why Are Girls with ADHD Overlooked, Underdiagnosed, and Underserved?" *Education Update* 12, no. 10 (June 2007): 11. EducationUpdate.com/archives/2007/JUN/html/speced-whyaregirls.html.

Hoza, Betsy, et al. "A Randomized Trial Examining the Effects of Aerobic Physical Activity on Attention-Deficit/Hyperactivity Disorder Symptoms in Young Children." *Journal of Abnormal Child Psychology* 43, no. 4 (May 2015): 655-667. doi.org/10.1007/s10802-014-9929-y.

Kabat-Zinn, Jon. *Full Catastrophe Living: Using the Wisdom of Your Body and Mind to Face Stress, Pain, and Illness.* New York, NY: Bantam, 2013.

Kennedy, Diana. "The ADHD Symptoms That Complicate and Exacerbate a Math Learning Disability." *ADDitude* magazine. Last modified September 11, 2020. ADDitudeMag.com/math-learning-disabilities-dyscalculia-adhd.

Littman, Ellen. "The Secret Lives of Girls With ADHD." *Attention* magazine, December 2012, 18-20. Accessed December 2019. CHADD .org/wp-content/uploads/2018/06/ATTN_12_12_Littman _Attention.pdf.

Morton, Jill. "Why Color Matters." Colorcom. December 2019. Colorcom.com/research/why-color-matters.

MTA Cooperative Group. "A 14-Month Randomized Clinical Trial of Treatment Strategies for Attention-Deficit/Hyperactivity Disorder." *Archives of General Psychiatry* 56, no. 12 (December 1999): 1073-86. doi.org/10.1001/archpsyc.56.12.1073.

Nadeau, Kathleen, Ellen Littman, and Patricia Quinn. *Understanding Girls with ADHD: How They Feel and Why They Do What They Do.* N.p.: Advantage Books, 2015.

Pacheco, Danielle. "ADHD and Sleep." SleepFoundation.org. Last modified January 15, 2021. Accessed November 2019. SleepFoundation.org /articles/adhd-and-sleep.

Quinn, Patricia, and Kathleen Nadeau. "Understanding Girls with AD/ HD—Part I." National Center for Gender Issues and AD/HD. Accessed November 2019.

Ratey, John. "Build Your Muscles, Build Your Brain." *ADDitude* magazine. Last modified January 3, 2021. ADDitudeMag.com /exercise-learning-adhd-brain.

Sadeh, Avi, Lee Pergamin, and Yair Bar-Haim. "Sleep in Children with Attention-Deficit Hyperactivity Disorder: A Meta-Analysis of Polysomnographic Studies." *Sleep Medicine Reviews* 10, no. 6 (December 2006): 381-398. doi.org/10.1016/j.smrv.2006.03.004.

Scherer, Priscilla. "Could Your Child Have Auditory Processing Disorder?" *ADDitude* magazine. Last modified November 23, 2020. ADDitudeMag.com/a-labor-to-listen-is-it-adhd-or-apd.

Skogli, Eric Winther, et al. "ADHD in Girls and Boys—Gender Differences in Co-Existing Symptoms and Executive Function Measures." *BMC Psychiatry* 13 (November 2013): 298. doi.org/10.1186/1471 -244X-13-298.

Understood Team. "ADHD and Perfectionism: What You Need to Know." Understood. Accessed November 2019. Understood.org/en /learning-thinking-differences/child-learning-disabilities/add-adhd /adhd-and-perfectionism.

Williams, Penny, and ADHD Editorial Board. "What Are the 3 Types of ADHD?" *ADDitude* magazine. Last modified January 3, 2021. ADDitudeMag.com/3-types-of-adhd.

INDEX

A

Accommodations, managing school, 42–43

Adderall, 51

ADDitude (magazine), 9, 26, 84, 95, 97

Additude–ADHD Support Group, 96

ADHD. *See* Attention deficit hyperactivity disorder (ADHD)

Adler Center for Research in Child Development and Psychopathology, 82

American Psychiatric Association (APA), 8, 9

American Psychological Association, 10

Anxiety
  signs of, 59–60
  tips for intervention, 60

Assistive technology, 27, 43

Attention (magazine), 62

Attention deficit hyperactivity disorder (ADHD), *ix–x. See also* Girls with ADHD
  early intervention, 10
  elementary school signs and challenges, 44–46
  gifts of, 78
  in girls, 6–10
  managing life at home, 39–41
  managing life at school, 41–43
  medications and, 49–52
  middle school signs and challenges, 46–49
  neurodevelopment disorder, 6
  puberty and, 49
  tips for parents, 30–31, 33
  tips for siblings, 31, 32
  type 1, 6, 23–24, 63
  type 2, 7, 24–25, 56, 63
  type 3, 8, 25, 62, 63
  understanding, 6–8

Auditory processing disorder (APD), 26

B

Balloon technique, 16

Bedtime, managing, 39–40

Behavioral strategies for parents, 11–20
  discipline, 14–17
  planning ahead, 17–20
  verbal cues, 11–14

C

Calendar
  color-coding, 43
  homework, 44–45
  planning, 78

Calm (app), 85

Calming strategies, 16–17

CHADD (Children and Adults with Attention-Deficit/Hyperactivity Disorder), 9, 50, 62, 96

Clonidine, 51

Cognitive behavioral therapy (CBT), 85

Color-coding, 43

Combined type of ADHD, 8, 25

CommonSenseMedia.org, 48

Concerta, 51

D

Daily schedule, checklists, 18–20

De-escalation ideas, 15–16

Depression
  anxiety and, 59–60
  tips for intervention, 60

Diagnostic and Statistical Manual of Mental Disorders (DSM-5), 8–9

Discipline
  calming strategies, 16–17
  de-escalation ideas, 15–16
  flexibility in, 31
  parents, 14–17
Distraction, 15, 24, 29, 43, 47
Distraction (Hallowell), 96
Doctors, treatment plan, 92
Dodson, William, 12
Dopamine, 49, 50
Dyscalculia, 28
Dysgraphia, 27
Dyslexia, 27

E

Early intervention, 10
Eating disorders
  girls with ADHD and, 60–62
  observing, 61
  tips for intervention, 61–62
Education, accommodations for, 42–43
Effective instructions, 11, 13–14
Elementary school, 53. *See also* School
  homework, 44–45
  socializing, 45–46
Emotions
  regulation, 29, 74
  regulation development, 76
Executive function
  creating time management
    systems, 76–77
  flexible thinking, 30, 74, 76
  helping girls develop skills, 75–78
  language development, 28–30
  modeling organization, 77–78
  organizing, 29, 73
  planning, 29, 72–73, 78
  prioritizing, 29, 72–73
  reducing forgetfulness, 77
  regulating emotions, 29, 74, 76
  self-monitoring, 75
  self-reflection, 30, 75

  skills, 29–30, 34, 71–75
  task completion, 76
  task initiation, 29, 73
  time management, 71–72
  working memory, 29–30, 74
Exercise
  girls with ADHD, 82–83
  parents, 87
Expectations
  holding onto unrealistic, 5–6
  managing, 20
  parents being clear with, 30, 31
The Explosive Child (Greene), 14, 88
Expressive language skills, 26–27

F

Facebook, 91, 96, 98
Family therapy, 85

G

Gender expectations, girls with ADHD
  and, 65–66
Girls with ADHD
  ADHD in, 6–10
  anxiety and depression, 59–60
  brain processing information, *ix*
  case of Georgie, 7, 25, 45, 66, 73
  case of Kiara, 8, 25, 32, 45, 56, 72–73
  case of Lexie, 7, 24, 32, 45, 72
  early intervention, 10
  eating disorders in, 60–62
  fostering self-esteem in, *x*, 55–58
  gender expectations and, 65–66
  impulse control in, 63–64
  internalizing problems, 56–57
  peer approval and acceptance, 65
  self-harm in, 62–63
  tips for intervention, 57–58
Google Calendar, 44, 73
Greene, Ross W., 14, 88
Gretzky, Wayne, 33
Guanfacine (Intuniv), 51

H

Headspace (app), 85
Homework, elementary school, 44–45
Hyperactive-impulsive type of ADHD (type 1), 6, 23–24, 63

I

Impulse control, girls with ADHD and, 63–64
Inattentive type ADHD (type 2), 7, 24–25, 56, 63
Individualized education plan (IEP), 8, 42, 52
Individuals with Disabilities Education Act (IDEA), 42
Instagram, 48
International Journal of Eating Disorders (journal), 60
Intervention, 10
    anxiety and depression, 60
    creating success wall, 58
    eating disorders, 61–62
    girls with ADHD, 57–58
    healthy friendships, 57
    identifying strengths, 58
    impulse control, 64
    modeling self-talk, 57
    self-awareness, 57–58
    self-esteem, 57–58
    self-harm, 63

J

Journal of Abnormal Child Psychology (journal), 83

L

Language development
    auditory processing, 26
    executive function, 28–30
    expressive and receptive skills, 26–27
    literacy development, 27–28

Learning disabilities
    dyscalculia, 28
    dysgraphia, 27
    dyslexia, 27
Life at home
    bedtime, 39–40
    mealtimes, 40
    playdates, 40–41
Literacy development
    dyscalculia, 28
    dysgraphia, 27
    dyslexia, 27
Littman, Ellen, *ix*, 57

M

McCabe, Jessica, 97
Managing ADHD
    elementary school, 44–46
    life at home, 39–41
    life at school, 41–43
    medications for, 49–52
    middle school, 46–49
Mealtimes, managing, 40
Medications
    ADHD and, 49–52
    benefits of, 50–51
    facts *vs.* myths, 50
    managing ADHD, 49–52
    potential side effects, 51–52
    science of, 50
    stimulants *vs.* non-stimulants, 51
Memory. *See* Working memory
Middle school, 53. *See also* School
    emerging sexuality, 49
    expectations, 46
    signs and challenges, 46–49
    socializing, 47
    social media and, 48
    tips for parents, 46–47
Mindfulness-based cognitive therapy (MBCT), 85

Mindfulness exercise, 89–90
Movement breaks, 43
MTA Cooperative Group, 51
Multitasking, 29–30, 75

N
Nadeau, Kathleen, *ix*
National Eating Disorders Association (NEDA), 61
NationalEatingDisorders.org, 61
National Suicide Prevention Lifeline, 62
Non-stimulant medications, 51
Non-suicidal self-injury (NSSI), 62
Norepinephrine, 49
Nutrition, 83

O
Organization
    modeling, 77–78
    skills, 29, 73

P
Parent(s)
    advocating for daughter, 42
    behavioral strategies for, 11–20
    calming strategies, 16–17
    de-escalation ideas, 15–16
    discipline, 14–17
    effective instructions, 13–14
    keeping things positive, 12
    peer interactions and, 65
    showering girls with praise, 13
    support group, 96
    tips for, 30–31, 33
    tips for elementary school, 44–45
    tips for middle school girls, 46–47
    treatment plan, 91
    verbal cues, 11–14
Parental care, 86–90
    ADHD and, 87–88
    burnout, 86
    care for the caretaker, 88

    exercise, 87
    hobbies, 87
    mindfulness exercise, 89–90
    skills training, 88
    support group, 87
    tips for being mindful, 89
Peer approval and acceptance, 65
Perfectionist/perfectionism, 10, 25
Planning
    skills, 29, 72–73
    teaching calendar use, 78
Planning ahead
    appropriate activities, 17–18
    managing expectations, 20
    visual schedules and checklists, 18–20
Playdates, managing, 40–41
Podcasts, 76, 96
Positivity, 11, 12
Praise, 11, 13
Prioritization, skills, 29, 72–73
Puberty, ADHD and, 49

Q
Quinn, Patricia, *ix*

R
Receptive language skills, 26–27
Rehabilitation Act, Section 504, 42, 52
Resources, 95–98
Restless leg syndrome, 82
Ritalin, 51
Routines, 14, 31
    bedtime, 39–40
    sleep, 81–82

S
School. *See also* Elementary school; Middle School
    accommodations for, 42–43
    advocating for your daughter, 42
    assignment breakdowns, 43

assistive technology, 43
color-coding, 43
elementary school, 44–46
IEP (individualized education plan)
    and 504 plan, 42
Individuals with Disabilities
    Education Act (IDEA), 42–43
managing life at, 41–43
middle school, 46–49
movement breaks, 43
study partner/peer tutoring, 42
workspaces, 43
The Secret Lives of Girls with ADHD
    (Littman), 57
Section 504 of Rehabilitation Act, 42, 52
Self-awareness, 57–58
Self-esteem
    fostering, 55–58
    internalizing struggles, 56–57
    interventions, 57–58
    late diagnosis and, 56
Self-harm, girls with ADHD and, 62–63
Self-reflection, 30, 75
Sensory breaks, 17, 43
Siblings, tips for, 31, 32
Sleep, girls with ADHD, 81–82
SLEEP (journal), 82
Sleep Research Society, 82
Snapchat, 48
Socializing
    elementary school, 45–46
    middle school, 47
Social media, 46, 48, 53
Special Education Parent Advisory
    Groups (SEPAG), 91
Stimulant-based medications, 51
Strattera, 51, 52
Stress management, 84
Success
    action plan for, 92–93
    exercise, 82–83

inclusive treatment plan and
    ADHD, 90–92
mindfulness exercise, 89–90
nutrition, 83
parental care, 86–90
sleep, 81–82
stress management, 84
supplements, 83–84
team of professionals for, 86
therapy and ADHD, 84–85
Suicide, 62–63
Supplements, 83–84
Support group, 87, 91, 96, 98

T

Tasks
    determination to finish, 76
    initiation, 29, 73
Teachers
    accommodations to request
        of, 42–43
    advocating for your daughter, 42
    homework, 44
    middle school expectations, 46
    peer interactions and, 65
    questions for, 92
    treatment plan, 91–92
TED talk, 97
Therapists, treatment plan, 92
Therapy
    ADHD and, 84–85
    cognitive behavioral therapy
        (CBT), 85
    family, 85
    mindfulness-based cognitive therapy
        (MBCT), 85
Thinking, flexible, 30, 74, 76
TikTok, 48
Time management
    creating systems, 76–77
    executive skill, 71–72

Treatment plan
    ADHD and, 90–92
    doctors, 92
    parents, 91
    teachers, 91–92
    therapists, 92

U

Understanding Girls with ADHD
    (Nadeau, Littman and Quinn), *ix*
Unrealistic expectations, 5–6

V

Vanderbilt ADHD Diagnostic Rating
    Scale, 8
Vyvanse, 51

W

Working memory
    accessing, 29–30, 74
    building, 75
    deficits, 28
    reducing forgetfulness, 77
World Health Organization, 62

Y

Yoga, 85, 87
Yoga video, 17
YouTube, 17, 58, 76, 87, 97

ABOUT THE AUTHOR

 **Allison K. Tyler, LCSW,** is a licensed clinical social worker who has specialized in working with children, teens, and adults with ADHD over the course of her 17-year career. She graduated from New York University with her master's in social work in 2003, has a postgraduate certificate in children and families from Royal Holloway University in London, and a bachelor of arts from Colby College.

Allison works in private practice and has developed a unique skills-based approach that she individualizes for each of her clients. When working with children and teens, Allison works in partnership with parents and also provides parent training and consultation services to schools. Allison has completed Dr. Ross W. Greene's advanced-level training in collaborative problem-solving and incorporates the tenets of his philosophy into all of her clinical work.

Allison lives in New Jersey with her loving and very British husband, Jonathan; their son, Callum; daughter, Celeste; their labradoodle, Ivy; and cat, Sylvester.

You can find more about Allison at ADHDStrategyMom.com.

Printed in the USA
CPSIA information can be obtained
at www.ICGtesting.com
LVHW011946241123
764718LV00014B/362